AF513491

For a good crop, adequate credit should be available to farmers in time. The target for agricultural credit in 2017-18 has been fixed at a record level of ₹ 10 lakh crore. We will take special efforts to ensure adequate flow of credit to the under-serviced areas, the Eastern States and Jammu & Kashmir. The farmers will also benefit from 60 days' interest waiver announced by Honourable Prime Minister in respect of their loans from the co-operative credit structure.

—Budget Speech 2017-2018 by Finance Minister Shri Arun Jaitley,
February 1, 2017

Agricultural Economy of India

Current Status and Issues

By

Malvika Singh

Assistant Professor,
Department of Political Science,
Shivaji College, University of Delhi

New Century Publications
New Delhi, India

NEW CENTURY PUBLICATIONS
4800/24, Bharat Ram Road,
Ansari Road, Daryaganj,
New Delhi - 110 002 (India)

Tel.: 011-2324 7798, 4358 7398, 6539 6605
Fax: 011-4101 7798
E-mail: indiatax@vsnl.com • info@newcenturypublications.com
www.newcenturypublications.com

Editorial office:
LG–7, Aakarshan Bhawan,
4754-57/23, Ansari Road, Daryaganj,
New Delhi – 110 002

Tel.: 011-4356 0919

Copyright © 2017 by the author

All rights reserved. No part of this book may be reproduced, stored in a retrieval system, or transmitted in any form or by any means, mechanical, photocopying, recording, or otherwise without the prior written permission of the publisher.

First Published: **2017**

ISBN: **978-81-7708-442-9**

Published by New Century Publications and printed at Salasar Imaging Systems, New Delhi.

Designs: Patch Creative Unit, New Delhi.

PRINTED IN INDIA

About the Book

Agriculture occupies a key position in the Indian economy. Though agriculture has now shrunk as a proportion of gross domestic product (GDP) to around 13 percent, it is a vital sector and provider of livelihood for 2/3rd of India's working population. Agriculture being a State subject, the bulk of public investment in agriculture takes place at the level of States and the Central Government supports the States as a catalyst. The nodal agency for development of agriculture in India is the Ministry of Agriculture and Farmers Welfare, Government of India.

Agricultural policy followed since Independence in 1947 can be broadly classified into three phases. Phase one, immediately after Independence, witnessed several institutional changes through land reforms and initiation of major irrigation projects. The second phase, since the mid-1960s, was aimed at increasing agricultural productivity to attain self-sufficiency in foodgrains through technological revolution and Government support for credit, marketing, and extension services. This was followed by the current phase, since the late 1980s, aimed at making agriculture more market-oriented.

Regrettably, Indian economy has been witnessing loss of dynamism in the agriculture and allied sectors in recent years. The sector, as a whole, has showed poor performance lately. Signs of agrarian distress are visible in parts of the country. The spate of suicides by farmers in some areas is the most disconcerting manifestation of this distress. Marginal and small farmers have borne the brunt of the adverse circumstances in agriculture. Concerned by the slow growth in the agriculture and allied sectors, the Government of India has launched a series of programmes/schemes in recent years to rejuvenate agriculture and improve farm income.

The present work explains and examines the key reform measures undertaken for the modernization of Indian agriculture. Challenges facing this vital sector of the economy are also set forth.

About the Author

Dr. Malvika Singh, is presently Assistant Professor, Department of Political Science, Shivaji College, University of Delhi. An alumnus of Lady Shri Ram College for Women, she is also a Research Fellow at the Developing Countries Research Centre (DCRC), University of Delhi. She earned her Doctorate of Philosophy in Political Science from the Centre for Political Studies, Jawaharlal Nehru University (JNU), New Delhi. She is also a guest faculty at many institutions including Pandit Deendayal Upadhay National Academy for Social Security, New Delhi.

Dr. Malvika is a regular participant in various national and international conferences, seminars and workshops. She has published several research papers in reputed journals. Her areas of academic interest and specialization are political philosophy, international political economy and gender studies.

Foreword

Agriculture in India has been envisioned as a provider of food and raw materials to the domestic population and the industries. Considering the poor rate of economic transition, agriculture remains a major provider of employment and income to a bulk of the population in the country. To achieve the above, the country initially concentrated on natural resource endowed regions. Agricultural growth in such regions stagnated; the second generation problems also started surfacing. There was also an urgency to make growth broad-based and therefore the emphasis shifted to rain-fed and dry regions. Of late, water—a critical resource for agriculture—became scarcer and the extension of the same required more investment. The governance related issue became more important and some regions remained difficult. Bundelkhand in Uttar Pradesh is an example. The historical backwardness of the region, accompanied with missed opportunities of extending public irrigation facilities made the region even more disadvantageous. The present book based on the field study in Mahoba, Banda, Hamirpur and Jhansi in Bundelkhand region of Uttar Pradesh presents the current situation in greater details.

The difficulties in region like Bundelkhand further aggravated with the trade liberalisation of the 1990s. With the opening up of trade, relative emphasis on instruments of development changes; market plays a more important role in economic development of a region. But a region with rudimentary and inter-locked markets creates further problems in agricultural development of the region. Demographic pressure without any significant progress in non-agricultural sectors made the region more unfavourable and the working population started migrating to different growth centres of the country for livelihood.

In this context, the present book provides an account of how small and marginal cultivators got trapped in a vicious circle of free market forces. This deliberates historical development of the region and its linkages with the current development in agriculture. This book will be useful to anyone interested in the process of understanding agricultural development in India.

Brajesh Jha
Professor and Head,
Agriculture Economics Unit,
Institute of Economic Growth,
Delhi - 110 007

Contents

Preface

Agriculture occupies a pivotal position in the Indian economy. Though agriculture has now shrunk as a proportion of gross domestic product (GDP) to around 13 percent, it is a vital sector and provider of livelihood for 2/3rd of India's working population. It is but natural that the problems of farmers are addressed with a sense of urgency. Agriculture being a State subject, the bulk of public investment in agriculture takes place at the level of States and the Central Government supports the States as a catalyst.

The nodal agency for development of agriculture in India is the Ministry of Agriculture and Farmers Welfare, Government of India. It has three departments: (a) Department of Agriculture, Co-operation and Farmers Welfare, (b) Department of Animal Husbandry, Dairying and Fisheries and (c) Department of Agricultural Research and Education.

Agricultural policy followed in India since Independence in 1947 can be broadly classified into three phases. Phase one, immediately after Independence, witnessed several institutional changes through land reforms and initiation of major irrigation projects. The second phase, since the mid-1960s, was aimed at increasing agricultural productivity to attain self-sufficiency in foodgrains through technological revolution and Government support for credit, marketing, and extension services. This was followed by the current phase, since the late 1980s, aimed at making agriculture more market-oriented.

Agricultural and allied products like cereals (mainly wheat and rice), tea, coffee, cashew, spices, tobacco and leather are important items of India's exports and hence foreign exchange earnings. Agriculture is also the source of raw material for agro-based industries including textiles, cigarettes, jute, sugar, paper, processed foodstuffs and *vanaspati*. Moreover, agricultural sector provides market for capital goods (tractors, pump sets and other agricultural machinery), inputs (fertilisers, insecticides), and light consumer goods. The nation has invested huge resources for the development of agriculture under various Five Year Plans.

Unfortunately, Indian economy has been witnessing loss of dynamism in the agriculture and allied sectors in recent years. The sector, as a whole, has showed poor performance lately. Signs of agrarian distress are visible in parts of the country. The spate of suicides by farmers in some areas is the most disconcerting manifestation of this distress. Marginal and small farmers have borne the brunt of the adverse circumstances in agriculture.

Concerned by the slow growth in the agriculture and allied sectors, the Government of India has launched a series of programmes/schemes in recent years to rejuvenate agriculture and improve farm income. These, inter alia, have included the following:

- *Rashtriya Krishi Vikas Yojana* (RKVY), 2007.
- Macro Management of Agriculture (MMA) Scheme.
- Extending Green Revolution to the Eastern States.
- Integrated Scheme of Oilseeds, Pulses, Oil Palm and Maize (ISOPOM).
- Support to State Extension Programmes for Extension Reforms.
- National Project on Promotion of Organic Farming (NPOF).
- Policy Framework for Agricultural Extension (PFAE).
- Agricultural Technology Management Agency (ATMA).
- *Parmparagat Krishi Vikas Yojana.*
- Organic Value Chain Development in North East Region.

Since 1991, India has witnessed a successful transition from a controlled, inward-looking, and slow growing economy to a liberalised and open economy that has now found a place amongst the fastest growing economies in the world. The liberalisation process which started in the early 1990s encompassed wide-ranging reform measures in the areas of industry, public finances, banking and insurance, foreign trade and exchange rate management. These reforms are aimed at reorientation of the economy from a centrally directed command and control economy to a market-oriented one in order to foster greater efficiency and growth. This has been done by introducing greater competition in the economy through progressive internal deregulation accompanied by external competition promoted by foreign direct investment and trade liberalisation.

Although agriculture is still the backbone of the Indian economy, at least in terms of employment, the impulses of reforms have been relatively less in scope and depth in this sector. It is noteworthy that reforms in agricultural sector were introduced only towards the end of the 1990s. Nevertheless, a series of policy initiatives have been undertaken in this sector as well. These include: (a) partial decontrol of fertiliser prices, (b) removal of bottlenecks in agricultural marketing, (c) relaxation of restrictions under the Essential Commodities Act, 1955, (d) introduction of forward trading in important commercial crops, (e) replacement of the Revamped Public Distribution System with Targeted Public Distribution System, (f) establishment of Rural Infrastructural Development Fund (RIDF) and (g) replacement of quantitative controls by tariff.

Still further, micro credit, routed through self-help groups (SHGs), has emerged as a visible credit channel to the poor as their access to conventional credit channels is constrained by the requirement of collateral and high transaction cost. The National Horticulture Mission was launched on April 1, 2005 to ensure end-to-end approach having backward and forward linkages covering research, production, post-harvest management, processing and marketing.

While there have been efforts—such as those to promote institutional credit to rural areas, improved access to inputs, subsidies on fertilisers and electricity, minimum support price etc.—these have not been fully successful in protecting the interest of the farmers in general, and small/marginal farmers in particular.

Increasing agricultural production with limited natural resources in a sustainable manner for ensuring food and nutritional security and providing income security to farmers are the major challenges before the Government. Moreover, accelerating the rate of growth of agricultural production must be seen as central to a more inclusive growth.

Acknowledgments

In the process of putting this book together, first and foremost I would like to thank God and my family, they made me believe how this true gift of writing is for me. I am particularly grateful to all my colleagues and students at University of Delhi and Developing Countries Research Centre, University of Delhi. I have also taken ideas in this book on road to several institutions of higher learning and libraries both in India and abroad.

I would also like to express my gratitude to many people who saw me through this book, to all those who provided support both intellectual and emotional, talked over things, read, wrote, offered comments allowed me to quote their remarks and assisted in the editing, proofreading and design.

This book is particularly the result of encouragement and belief my mother has in me. I can barely find words to express all the wisdom, love and support my mother have given me.

Last and not the least, I beg forgiveness of all those who have been with me over the course of the years and whom I have failed to mention.

January 2017 **Malvika Singh**

1

Economic Reforms and Agriculture in India

The political and economic scene in India is greatly different today from what existed during British rule. Before 1947, India was a dependency of the United Kingdom and consisted of British India, and the Princely States. It encompassed the entire area which now forms the four countries of India, Pakistan, Burma, and Bangladesh. The Princely States enjoyed internal financial autonomy and therefore did not form part of the public finances. They had separate budgets and separate sources of revenue. Neither there was any plan of economic development nor was there any attempt to build a welfare society.

Presently, India is an independent country and it includes the former Princely States but excludes the other three countries mentioned above.

1.1 Agricultural Situation at the Time of Independence

Independence was gained on August 15, 1947 at the cost of partition of the country which cut across its economic and cultural unity and the centuries of common life to which all the communities had contributed. Whatever might have been the political justification of partition, its economic consequences were disastrous. Regions which had functioned for centuries on a complementary basis were suddenly cut asunder. After partition, India and Pakistan had each points of advantages and disadvantages. In general, it may be said that while India was much stronger at that time in industrial production and mineral resources, Pakistan had some advantage in agricultural resources, especially foodstuffs. In fact, the complementary character of their economies was much deeper than is indicated by this generalisation.

India inherited a dismal economy from the British rulers in

1947. It was characterised by poor technological and scientific capabilities, and limited and lop-sided industrialisation. Agricultural sector exhibited features of feudal and semi-feudal institutions, resulting in low productivity. Means of transport and communications were underdeveloped, educational and health facilities inadequate and social security measures virtually non-existent. Poverty was rampant and unemployment widespread, both making for low general standard of living. In short, the country was backward in every respect.

India was faced with three formidable problems, viz. severe food shortage, mounting inflation and the influx of refugees in the wake of partition of the country. These problems had to be addressed on an urgent basis. Thus, the first task of Indian Government in the immediate post-Independence period was to initiate growth process in agriculture on modern lines. Modernization of agriculture was required both in terms of technological and institutional changes. Abolition of intermediaries in agriculture, like *zamindars* and *jagirdars*, was accomplished soon after Independence.

The food situation caused anxiety and conditions became worse in large parts of the Madras presidency following the failure of the monsoon. Steps were taken to make additional supplies available but the position was difficult until the new harvest came on the market. The country had just weathered a serious threat of a breakdown of its rationing system. The results of the *Grow More Food Campaign* were on the whole disappointing.

The reliance on the import of foodgrains imposed a heavy strain on the finances of the Government. The exchange difficulty of the country was almost entirely due to the import of foodgrains on a large scale. The meagre exchange resources available to the country were consumed by the purchase of foodstuffs from abroad with the result that the Government had to impose the most stringent restrictions on the import of many essential articles. The various steps necessary for making the country self-sufficient in foodgrains claimed the highest priority.

First Five Year Plan (1951-52 to 1955-56) accorded pride of place to programmes for agriculture and community development. This was a natural priority in a plan seeking to raise the standard of living of the mass of the people, especially in rural areas, but it was also justified in the special circumstances of shortages and inflation which existed when the plan was formulated. The Plan envisaged substantial increases in agricultural production for foodgrains as well as for commercial crops. The targets proposed in the Plan were realised through development programmes relating to major and minor irrigation works, extension of cultivation, reclamation and intensive farming based on the application of the results of research.

Considerable stress was laid on the conservation of existing resources, in particular, of forests and the soil. Diversification and expansion of the rural economy was sought through emphasis on the development of dairying and horticulture and through the growth of village industries, wherever possible, with the aid of power and improved tools. Land resources were supplemented by the resources of sea and river and, therefore, the Plan provided for a new and extensive programme for the development of fisheries.

The overall results of the Plan were quite satisfactory. National income over the Plan period increased by around 18 percent. Foodgrains production went up by 20 percent; the output of cotton and of major oilseeds showed an improvement of 45 and 8 percent respectively. Over 6 million acres of land was brought under irrigation through major works; another 10 million acres benefited through smaller works. With the increased supplies of fertilizers and seeds and the further expansion of the national extension movement, sound foundations were laid for future development of the agricultural sector.

1.2 Initiation of Economic Reforms

For almost three decades after Independence, development pattern of India was characterised by strong centralised planning, government ownership of basic and key industries, excessive regulation and control of private enterprise, trade protectionism through tariff and non-tariff barriers and a cautious and selective approach towards foreign capital. It was quota, permit and license regime guided and controlled by a bureaucracy trained in colonial style. Indian economy grew at an average rate of 3.5 percent per annum during the first 30 years (1950-80) of planned economic development.

This so-called inward-looking, import substitution strategy of economic development began to be widely questioned with the beginning of 1980s. Policy makers started realising the drawbacks of this strategy which inhibited competitiveness and efficiency and produced a much lower rate of growth than expected.

Consequently, economic reforms were set in motion, though on a modest scale, when controls on industries were reduced by the 1985 industrial policy. After assuming power at the Centre, the Government of Prime Minister Rajiv Gandhi introduced a series of measures, through its 1985 industrial policy, to reduce control on industries, particularly large industries. These measures, described as New Economic Policy, coincided with the policy framework of the Seventh Five Year Plan (1985-90).

Furthermore, a number of policy and procedural changes were introduced in 1985 and 1986 aimed at increasing productivity, reducing costs and improving quality. The emphasis was on opening the domestic market to increased competition and preparing the Indian industry to stand on its own in the face of international competition. The technological and managerial modernisation of industry was stressed as the key instrument for increasing productivity and improving our competitiveness in the world.

Economic reforms started in right earnest when the Government of Prime Minister Narsimha Rao announced a new industrial policy in the Indian Parliament on July 24, 1991. The new policy introduced radical changes "to unshackle the Indian industrial economy from the cobwebs of unnecessary bureaucratic controls". Since then, it is liberalisation, privatisation and globalisation all the way and the process is underway. In the new liberalised industrial and trade environment, the Government is progressively assuming the role of a promoter, facilitator and catalytic agent instead of a regulator and controller of economic activities.

The liberalisation process which started in the early 1990s encompassed wide-ranging reform measures in the areas of industry, public finances, banking and insurance, foreign trade and exchange rate management. The purpose of these economic reforms was two-fold: (a) to restore macroeconomic stability on both domestic and external fronts, and (b) to place the economy on a higher growth path through enhanced levels of investment, and improvements in productivity, efficiency and competitiveness.

Economic reforms in the Indian economy have taken a variety of forms.

1. Industrial deregulation.
2. Liberalisation of foreign direct investment.
3. Trade liberalization.
4. Enactment of electricity legislation.
5. Deregulation of telecom sector.
6. Lowering of rates of direct and indirect taxes.
7. Dilution of government holding in public sector undertakings.
8. Financial sector reforms (banking, insurance and capital market).

Economic reforms are aimed at reorientation of the centrally controlled economy to a market-oriented one in order to foster greater efficiency and growth. This is being done by introducing greater competition in the economy through progressive internal deregulation accompanied by external competition promoted by foreign direct investment and trade liberalisation. No area of the Indian economy has been as much influenced by the impulses of reforms as the industrial sector.

1.3 Reforms in the Agricultural Sector

Although agriculture is still the backbone of the Indian economy, at least in terms of employment, the impulses of reforms have been relatively less in scope and depth in this sector. Reforms in agricultural sector were introduced only towards the end of the 1990s. Nevertheless, a series of policy initiatives have been undertaken in this sector as well. These include: (a) partial decontrol of fertiliser prices, (b) removal of bottlenecks in agricultural marketing, (c) relaxation of restrictions under the Essential Commodities Act, 1955, (d) introduction of forward trading in important commercial crops, (e) replacement of the Revamped Public Distribution System with Targeted Public Distribution System, (f) establishment of Rural Infrastructural Development Fund, and (g) replacement of quantitative controls by tariff.

Micro credit, routed through self-help groups (SHGs), has emerged as a visible credit channel to the poor as their access to conventional credit channels is constrained by the requirement of collateral and high transaction cost. India has adopted a multi-agency approach for the development of its micro-finance programme. All the major credit institutions, *viz.* commercial banks, co-operative banks, regional rural banks (RRBs) along with non-governmental organizations (NGOs) have been associated with the micro-finance programme. The role of the delivering agents and their interface has led to alternative models of micro-finance.

National Horticulture Mission, launched on April 1, 2005, aims to ensure end-to-end approach having backward and forward linkages covering research, production, post-harvest management, processing and marketing. On July 28, 2000, Government of India announced a National Agriculture Policy to include this vital sector of the economy in the ambit of economic reforms. National Commission on Farmers (NCF) under the Chairmanship of M.S. Swaminathan was set up in 2004 to suggest an action plan for farmers and farm sector. The Commission submitted five Reports between December

2005 and October 2006.

The Union Finance Minister, in his budget speech for the year 2000-01, announced a proposal to introduce a new social security scheme for agricultural workers called the *Khetihar Mazdoor Bima Yojana*. The initiative taken by the Government in introducing the scheme was widely welcomed. The scheme was launched on the May 18, 2001. It has been described as the first ever scheme for the welfare of the farm workers and a step towards meeting the social security needs of agricultural workers.

In the area of rural development, the most important development has been the enactment and implementation of the Mahatma Gandhi National Rural Employment Guarantee Act (MGNREGA), 2005. The objective of the MGNREGA is to enhance the livelihood security of the people in rural areas by guaranteeing 100 days of wage employment in a financial year to a rural household whose members volunteer to do unskilled manual work. The Act further aims at creating durable assets and strengthening the livelihood resource base of the rural poor. The choice of works suggested in the Act address causes of chronic poverty like drought, deforestation, soil erosion, etc. so that the process of employment generation is on a sustainable basis.

Rural Infrastructure Development Fund (RIDF) was set up under National Bank for Agriculture and Rural Development (NABARD) in 1995-96 to provide loans to State Governments and State-owned corporations for expeditious completion of on-going rural infrastructure projects. Under the scheme, commercial banks contribute to the Fund on the basis of their shortfall in their lending to the priority sectors/agriculture.

1.4 Assessment of Economic Reforms

The process of economic reforms in India initiated in 1991 seems irreversible. There is enough evidence that Government is withdrawing, though gradually, as a controller and licenser of private activity and allowing competition and market forces to guide investment decisions.

After the reforms, the Indian economy has been growing faster than its historical growth rate. Tenth Five Year Plan (2002-07) recorded annual growth rate of 7.2 percent and the Eleventh Five Year Plan (2007-12) achieved 7.9 percent growth rate per annum. It is now widely agreed that the Indian economy is capable of achieving high growth rates in response to the implementation of appropriate and timely economic reform policies. India is now Asia's third largest economy and has the world's eighth largest foreign exchange reserves.

Technology, competition, and benchmarking to the best international practices have to be the driving force of India's development efforts. Technology is getting upgraded rapidly and competition in the market place has become fierce. The vibrant IT industry is contributing immensely by providing information about latest technology and international business practices.

With quantitative restrictions on imports removed, customs duties progressively lowered, and foreign investment, both direct and portfolio, liberalised, integration of India into the global economy is progressing fast. Buoyant export performance, a surplus in the current account, and the strong balance of payments position demonstrate the success of the country in this integration process.

India's gradual and cautious approach to economic reforms has proved well-founded and the country is placed on a firm footing for future forays into domestic and global economic activities. When the Indian economy was opened to external competition in the early 1990s, many feared decline of domestic companies which had enjoyed protection through high tariff and non-tariff walls for about half a century since Independence. These fears were true but short-lived. After facing global competition for about a decade, Indian industry is emerging much stronger to find its rightful place not only in the domestic market, but also in foreign lands.

Unfortunately, economic reforms of the last 20 years have

not paid adequate attention to the social sector (health, education etc.). There is a feeling in some quarters that the industrial growth of India is becoming elite-oriented by registering relatively large increase in the production of electronics items, beverages, cosmetics, motor cars, refrigerators, and finer variety of textiles.

The new Government at the Centre, which took charge in May 2014, under the dynamic leadership of Prime Minister Shri Narendra Modi has a vision to make India a modern and vibrant economy. Policies and programmes to rejuvenate the economy have already been announced in this regard. These have included, inter alia, Start-up India Initiative, 2016, eBiz Project, Make in India Campaign, Stand-Up India Scheme, Ease of Doing Business, India Aspiration Fund (IAF), Atal Innovation Mission (AIM), India Inclusive Innovation Fund (IIIF), Digital India, Smart Cities Mission and permission to set up payment banks.

2

Agricultural Productivity and Areas of Concern

Agricultural policy followed since Independence can be broadly classified into three phases. Phase one, immediately after independence, witnessed several institutional changes through land reforms and initiation of major irrigation projects. The second phase, since the mid-1960s, was aimed at increasing agricultural productivity to attain self-sufficiency in foodgrains through technological revolution and public support to credit, marketing, extension etc. This was followed by the current phase, since the late 1980s, aimed at making agriculture more market-oriented.

Although Indian agriculture is way back compared to the levels in developed countries, some notable developments have occurred over the post-Independence period. Large areas which suffered from repeated failures of rainfall have received irrigation, new crops have come to occupy a significant position in the country's production and trade, agricultural and the industrial economies in the country now exert a powerful influence on one another, problems of rural indebtedness and the exploitative practices of the village moneylenders are much less, and finally there is already in the countryside an awakening and a desire for improved standard of living.

The development of the agricultural sector depends, to a large extent, on such core industries as power, petroleum, fertilisers and machine tools. Thus, there is inter-dependence between agriculture and industry. Two major components of agricultural development strategy have been: (a) subsidies on inputs, and (b) minimum support price for output.

2.1 Role of Agriculture in the Indian Economy

Agricultural sector occupies a key position in the Indian

economy. It provides employment to about 65 percent of the working population of India. It is imperative that the problems of farmers are addressed with a sense of urgency. Agriculture being a State subject, the bulk of public investment in agriculture takes place at the level of States and the Central Government supports the States as a catalyst.

Agricultural products like cereals (mainly rice), tea, coffee, cashew, spices, tobacco and leather are important items of India's exports and hence foreign exchange earnings. Agriculture is also the source of raw material for agro-based industries including textiles, cigarettes, jute, sugar, paper, processed foodstuffs and *vanaspati*.

Moreover, agricultural sector provides market for capital goods (tractors, pump sets and other agricultural machinery), inputs (fertilisers, insecticides), and light consumer goods. The nation has invested huge resources for the development of agriculture under various plans.

The development of the agricultural sector depends, to a large extent, on such core industries as power, petroleum, fertilisers and machine tools. Thus, there is inter-dependence between agriculture and industry.

Agriculture sector is vital for the food and nutritional security of the nation. Compared to other countries, India faces a greater challenge, since with only 2.3 percent share in world's total land area, it has to ensure food security of its population which is about 17.5 percent of world population. This leads to excessive pressure on land and fragmentation of land holdings.

Agriculture being a state subject, the primary responsibility for increasing agriculture production, enhancing productivity, and exploring the vast untapped potential of the sector rests with the State Governments. However, in order to supplement the efforts of the State Governments, a number of Centrally-sponsored and Central Sector schemes are being implemented for enhancing agricultural production and productivity in the country and increasing the income of the farming community.

2.2 Low Productivity of Indian Agriculture

Indian agriculture was backward and stagnant at the time of Independence. Ever since the launching of the First Five Year Plan (1951-56), agricultural sector has received the prime attention of the Government in the overall strategy of economic development. As a result, farm productivity has increased over the years and the country has achieved high degree of self-sufficiency in terms of foodgrains and raw material for agro-based industries (Table 2.1). Although per hectare yield of major crops has increased over the years yet it is far below the international levels (Table 2.2). This scenario calls for an examination of the causes of low productivity of agriculture in India.

Table 2.1: Trends in the Productivity of Indian Agriculture: Selected Years

(yield per hectare/kg.)

Crop	1980-81	1990-91	2000-01	2010-11	2015-16
Rice	1,336	1,740	1,901	2,240	2,404
Wheat	1,630	2,281	2,708	2,938	3,093
Coarse cereals	695	900	1,027	1,528	1,590
Pulses	473	578	544	689	652

Source: Reserve Bank of India, *Handbook of Statistics on Indian Economy*, 2015-16, Table 22 (excerpted).

Table 2.2: Crop Yield Comparison: India versus the World

Yield in kg. per hectare (2012)

Crop	India Highest Yield (State)	World Highest yield
Paddy	3,952 (Punjab)	6,661 (China)
Wheat	5,017 (Punjab)	7,360 (UK)
Maize	5,372 (Tamil Nadu)	8,858 (USA)
Chickpeas	1,439 (Andhra Pradesh	1,663 (Ethiopia)
Cotton	750 (Punjab)	1,920 (Australia)
Rapeseed/Mustard Seed	1,723 (Gujarat)	3,588 (UK)

Source; Government of India, *Economic Survey*, 2014-15, Volume I, Chapter 1, Table 1.1.

Statistical evidence suggests that farm productivity in India is low as compared to other countries of the world. The low productivity of the agricultural sector is attributable to a host of technological and institutional factors.

The central challenge of Indian agriculture is low productivity, evident in modest average yields, especially in pulses. India happens to be the major producer and consumer of pulses, which is one of the major sources of protein for the population. India has low yields comparable to most countries. Imports cannot be the main source for meeting domestic demand for pulses. Therefore, policy must incentivise movement of resources towards production of pulses.

The production pattern for pulses is very different from other crops. Not only is most of the land dedicated to growing pulses in each state unirrigated, but the national output of pulses comes predominantly from un-irrigated land. In contrast, a large share of output in wheat, rice and sugarcane—in Punjab, Haryana and UP—is from irrigated land. In water scarce Maharashtra, all sugarcane is grown on irrigated land. Meeting the high and growing demand for pulses in the country will require large increases in pulses production on irrigated land, but this will not occur if agriculture policies continue to focus largely on cereals and sugarcane.

While there have been efforts—such as those to promote institutional credit to rural areas, improved access to inputs, subsidies on fertilisers and electricity, minimum support price etc.—these have not been fully successful in protecting the interest of the farmers in general, and small/marginal farmers in particular. Small/marginal farmers have inadequate access to: (a) information, (b) agencies promoting technological change, (c) co-operative networks and related organisations and (d) plethora of governmental interventions. This is significant since, in any case, these farmers are less well placed to take advantage of the markets.

The negative consequences of low agriculture yields extend from precarious incomes of farmers to large tracts of land locked in low value agriculture, despite growing demands for high value products such as fruits, vegetables, livestock products because of consumption diversification with rising incomes and urbanization.

2.3 Declining Share of Agriculture in GDP

The composition of national income has changed steadily over the planning era. While the share of agriculture and allied activities in the gross domestic product (GDP) has declined, that of the tertiary sector has increased. The expansion of services has not only been conducive for employment generation but also for better efficiency of the system and better quality of life. As a result of significant fall in the share of agriculture in GDP, the aggregate GDP has become relatively less sensitive to fluctuations in agricultural performance.

Highlighting the changes in the sectoral composition of GDP over the years, the *Economic Survey*, 2011-12 observed, "The structure of the economy has also undergone significant changes over time. Between 1950-51 and 1980-81, the industrial sector registered a higher growth rate than the services sector. The converse has been the case since then. This resulted in the share of the industry sector in GDP increasing by around 9 percentage points from 16.6 percent to 25.9 percent during the period from 1950-51 to 1980-81. The share of the services sector increased from 30.3 percent in 1950-51 to 38 percent in 1980-81. It started growing rapidly thereafter and this phenomenon became more pronounced in the 1990s. Consequently, since 1980-81, the share of the industry sector has remained in the range of 26 to 28 percent of GDP, while the entire decline in share of agriculture has been balanced by an increase in share of the services sector. Thus, the resilience of the economy to shocks owes to the services sector which has the largest share and most consistent growth performance". [1]

The Document further noted, "Notwithstanding the declining trend in agriculture's share in GDP, the importance of the sector to the economy is best understood with reference to its share in employment and in terms of its criticality for macroeconomic stability. While the former was well known, the latter became manifest with rising growth in incomes since the mid-2000s. Hence, growth in agriculture and allied sectors remains an important objective and a 'necessary condition' for inclusive growth". [2]

The changes in relative shares of various sectors in GDP are shown in Table 2.3.

Table 2.3: Changes in the Sectoral Composition of GDP

Year	Agriculture	Industry	Services
1950-51	53.1	16.6	30.3
1960-61	48.7	20.5	30.8
1970-71	42.3	24.0	33.8
1980-81	36.1	25.9	38.0
1990-91	29.6	27.7	42.7
2000-01	22.3	27.3	50.4
2012-13	13.9	27.3	58.8
2013-14*	13.9	26.1	59.9

* Provisional.

Source: Government of India, *Economic Survey*, 2013-14, p. 6.

2.4 Eleventh Five Year Plan (2007-12) on Agriculture

Expressing concern on agricultural crisis and outlining strategy to regain agricultural dynamism, the Approach Paper on Eleventh Five Year Plan released by the Government in November 2006 observed, "One of the major challenges of the 11th Plan will be to reverse the deceleration in agricultural growth from 3.2 percent observed between 1980 and 1996-97 to a trend average of around 2.0 percent subsequently. This deceleration is the root cause of the problem of rural distress that has surfaced in many parts of the country and reached crisis levels in some. Low farm incomes due to inadequate productivity growth have often combined with low prices of output and with lack of credit at reasonable rates to push many farmers into crippling debt. Even otherwise, uncertainties seem to have increased (regarding prices, quality of inputs and also weather and pests) which, coupled with unavailability of proper extension and risk insurance have led farmers to despair. This has also led to widespread distress migration, a rise in the number of female headed households in rural areas and a general increase in women's work burden and vulnerability. In 2004-05, women accounted for 34 percent of principal and 89 percent of subsidiary workers in agriculture, higher than in any previous round of the National Sample Survey.

The crisis of agriculture is not a purely distributional one arising out of the special problems of small and marginal farmers and landless labour. In fact, agricultural deceleration is affecting farms of all sizes. To reverse this trend, corrective policies must not only focus on the small and marginal farmers who continue to deserve special attention, but also on middle and large farmers who suffer from productivity stagnation arising from a variety of constraints.

It is vital to increase agricultural incomes as this sector still employs nearly 60 percent of our labour force. A measure of self-sufficiency is also critical for ensuring food security. A second green revolution is urgently needed to raise the growth rate of agricultural GDP to around 4 percent. This is not an easy task since actual growth of agricultural GDP, including forestry and fishing, is likely to be below 2 percent for the Tenth Plan period. The challenge posed, therefore, is to at least double the rate of agricultural growth and to do so recognising demographic realities, particularly the increasing role of women". [3]

Outlining its strategy to raise agricultural output, the Plan document stated, "The Eleventh Plan strategy to raise agricultural output will be based on the following elements:

1. Double the rate of growth of irrigated area;
2. Improve water management, rain water harvesting and watershed development;
3. Reclaim degraded land and focus on soil quality;

4. Bridge the knowledge gap through effective extension;
5. Diversify into high value outputs, fruits, vegetables, flowers, herbs and spices, medicinal plants, bamboo, bio-diesel etc., but with adequate measures to ensure food security;
6. Promote animal husbandry and fishery;
7. Provide easy access to credit at affordable rates;
8. Improve the incentive structure and functioning of markets; and
9. Refocus on land reforms issues. [4]

2.5 Oilseeds/Edible Oils: Areas of Concern

The success the country achieved in raising production of foodgrains, sugar, fruits, vegetables and various plantation crops perhaps lulled the country into believing that the shortfall in oilseeds and pulses could likewise be successfully addressed.

The Technology Mission on Oilseeds (1986) achieved some initial success but continued expansion in population caused demand for oils to rise which the domestic output was unable to meet. Edible oil is an essential commodity, more so when a large majority of Indians are vegetarians and animal fats cannot be a substitute. Imports meet almost half the country's demand for edible oils.

Domestic production of three principal oil crops—groundnut, mustard and soyabean—suffer from following limitations: (a) lack of any genetic advance in technology in evolving high productivity seeds, (b) compulsion of raising oilseeds on unirrigated soils, (c) low productivity per hectare which can never match rice/wheat productivity levels even if grown on irrigated soil, and (d) high risk in losing production due to extreme sensitivity to adverse weather (frost/hailstorm) especially in case of mustard crop.

Unlike rice, wheat, sugar, bajra, jowar and cotton, farmers do not and cannot raise oilseeds as principal crop because of extreme risk factor. It is a supplementary cash crop and a proverbial gamble amidst weather uncertainty.

Diversion of area from foodgrains to oilseeds is widely

talked about and the key to this diversion is thought to lie in raising minimum support price (MSP) of oilseeds to provide oilseed growers a comparative price advantage relative to rice and wheat. Unfortunately this is unlikely to help as long as yield rates in oilseeds are so low relative to rice and wheat. Doubling or even tripling the MSP of oilseeds will not match their gross return per hectare vis-à-vis foodgrains.

Given the current low productivity levels in groundnut, mustard and soyabean, and the limitations to raising productivity levels, the country's dependence on imports to meet almost half of its requirements is unavoidable. Doubling of international price in 2002 caused little or no reduction in Indian imports which is evidence of inelasticity of demand. High import duties too had little effect on imported volumes. Improvements in yield rates and favourable pricing policy together can at best make only a marginal impact. Dependence on large volume of imports is bound to continue.

2.6 Post-harvest Losses

A comprehensive nation-wide quantitative assessment of harvest and post-harvest losses for 46 agricultural produces was carried out by the Department of Agricultural Research and Education of the Ministry of Agriculture, Government of India to estimate the extent of harvest and post-harvest losses. This assessment included five cereals, four pulses, six oilseeds, eight fruits, eight vegetables, sugarcane, four seed spices, three plantation crops, milk, meat, inland and marine fish, poultry meat and eggs. To assess these losses, data were collected through integrated stratified multistage survey design from 106 randomly selected districts of the country representing all targeted agricultural produces. Two blocks from each district and five villages from each block were randomly selected as second and third stage sampling units.

Finally, ten farmers from each village were taken for the assessment. This assessment covered 14 out of 15 agro-climatic zones (Island region agro-climatic zone was not included). The data were collected through enquiry as well as actual observations. Estimates obtained through both procedures were combined by assigning appropriate weighing factors before arriving at final estimate of losses for a commodity. The operations considered for assessment of losses were harvesting, collection, threshing, grading/sorting, winnowing/cleaning, drying, packaging, transportation, and storage depending upon the commodity. The post-harvest losses in cereals, pulses, oilseeds, fruits, vegetables, spices, condiments (plantation crops) are shown in Table 2.4.

Table 2.4: Post-harvest Losses of Select Agricultural Outputs in India

S. No.	Produce	Loss in percent
1	Cereals	3.9-6.0
2	Pulses	4.3-6.1
3	Oilseeds	2.2-10.1
4	Fruits	5.8-18.0
5	Vegetables	6.8-12.5
6	Spices	3.6-6.8
7	Condiments (Plantation Crops)	0.6-6.9

Source: Government of India, Ministry of Agriculture, Department of Agricultural Research and Education, *Annual Report*, 2010-11, p. 57.

To sum up, Indian economy is witnessing the slowing of agriculture at a time when the rest of the economy is growing at unprecedented rates. The sector, as a whole, has showed poor performance in the recent years. Agricultural growth rate has declined and foodgrains production has virtually stagnated. Signs of agrarian distress are visible in some years. The spate of suicides by farmers in many areas is the most disconcerting manifestation of this distress. Marginal and small farmers have borne the brunt of the adverse circumstances in agriculture.

As regards the performance of agricultural sector in recent Plans, the Approach Paper to Twelfth Five Year Plan (2012-17) observed, "A weakness in the economic performance thus far is that growth in the farm sector (agriculture and allied activities), though better than in the Tenth Plan, remains short of the 4.0 percent Plan target. The farm sector has grown at an average rate of around 3.2 percent during the first four years of the Eleventh Plan and assuming conditions remain favourable in 2011, the average farm sector growth in the Eleventh Plan period may be a little over 3.0 percent. This is a marked improvement from the average growth of about 2.0 percent during the Tenth Plan period. Still, with half of our population dependent on agriculture and allied activities, we need faster farm sector growth to benefit poor farmers, many of whom are women. The below target growth in this sector is one of the reasons for increase in food prices over the last two years". [5]

While agriculture no longer dominates the Indian economy in terms of national output, it is still the most important in terms of employment. In other words, declining share of income has not been accompanied by an equivalent decline in employment. It is a classic case of lop-sided structural transformation.

Accelerating the rate of growth of agricultural production is seen as central to a more inclusive growth.

Similarly, micro credit, routed through self-help groups (SHGs), has emerged as a visible credit channel to the poor as their access to conventional credit channels is constrained by the requirement of collateral and high transaction costs.

Against the backdrop of the burgeoning demand of population for foodgrains, degrading natural resource base, emerging concerns of climate change and other challenges, the Government has focused on mobilizing higher investment in agriculture, bridging yield gaps that exist across the states/regions, timely and adequate supply of quality inputs, and providing adequate support services to the farmers to make agriculture a remunerative vocation on a sustainable basis. Increasing agricultural production with limited natural resources in a sustainable manner for ensuring food and nutritional security and providing income security to farmers are the major challenges before the Government.

However, dependence on agriculture remains unchanged among the rural self-employed whose average farm size continues to decline with population growth. This is also an ageing, more feminised population, whose educated young members are less likely to want to stay in farming. The viability of farm enterprise, mostly small farms, must therefore be a special area of focus.

Endnotes

1. Government of India, *Economic Survey,* 2011-12, p. 8.
2. Ibid., p. 9.
3. Government of India, Planning Commission, *An Approach to the Eleventh Five Year Plan*, November 2006, p. 5.
4. Ibid., p. 23.
5. Government of India, Planning Commission, *An Approach to the Twelfth Five Year Plan*, October 2011, p. 7.

3

Institutional Set-up and Support for Agriculture

Being the biggest source of employment, agriculture holds a position of basic importance in any programme/scheme of economic development in India.

3.1 Ministry of Agriculture and Farmers Welfare

The nodal agency for development of agriculture in India is the Ministry of Agriculture and Farmers Welfare, Government of India.

3.1.1 Departments of the Ministry: It has three departments: (a) Department of Agriculture, Co-operation and Farmers Welfare, (b) Department of Animal Husbandry, Dairying and Fisheries and (c) Department of Agricultural Research and Education.

A. Department of Agriculture, Co-operation and Farmers Welfare: It deals with such matters as crops, horticulture, seeds, integrated nutrient management, plant protection, mechanization and technology, agriculture marketing, information technology, drought management, and agricultural census.

B. Department of Animal Husbandry, Dairying and Fisheries: This Department is responsible for matters relating to livestock production, preservation, protection and improvement of stocks, dairy development, matters relating to the Delhi Milk Scheme and the National Dairy Development Board. It also looks after all matters pertaining fisheries, which includes inland and marine sectors and matters related to the National Fisheries Development Board.

The Department advises the State Governments/Union Territories in the formulation of policies and programmes in the field of animal husbandry, dairy development and fisheries. The main focus of the activities is on: (a) development of requisite infrastructure in States/UTs for improving animal productivity, (b) promoting infrastructure for handling, processing and marketing of milk and milk products, (c) preservation and protection of livestock through provision of health care, (d) strengthening of central livestock farms (cattle, sheep and poultry) for development of superior germplasm for distribution to States and (e) expansion of aquaculture in fresh and brackish water, development of marine fisheries infrastructure and post-harvest operations and welfare of fisherfolk etc.

C. Department of Agricultural Research and Education (DARE): DARE coordinates and promotes agricultural research and education in the country. DARE provides the necessary government linkages for the Indian Council of Agricultural Research (ICAR), the premier research organisation with a scientific strength of about 25,000 and a countrywide network of 49 Institutes, 6 National Bureaux, 18 National Research Centres, 24 Project Directorates, 89 All-India Co-ordinated Research Projects and 45 Agriculture Universities spread all over the country.

DARE is the nodal agency for international co-operation in the area of agricultural research and education in India. It liaises with foreign governments, UN, and other multilateral agencies for cooperation in various areas of agricultural research. It also coordinates admissions of foreign students in various Indian agriculture universities/ICAR Institutes.

The major functions of DARE are the following:

1. To look after all aspects of the agricultural research and Education (including horticulture, natural resources management, agriculture engineering, agricultural extension, animal science, economic statics and marketing and fisheries) involving coordination between the central and state agencies.
2. To attend all matters relating to Indian Council of Agricultural Research.
3. To attend all matters concerning the development of new

technology in agriculture, horticulture, natural resources management, agriculture engineering, agricultural extension, animal science, economic statistics and marketing and fisheries, including such functions as plant and animal introduction and exploration and soil and land use survey and planning.

4. International co-operation in the field of agricultural research and education including relations with foreign and international agricultural research and educational institutions and organisations, including participation in international conferences, associations and other bodies dealing with agricultural research and education and follow-up decisions at such international conferences etc.
5. Fundamental, applied and operational research and higher education including co-ordination of such research and higher education in agriculture including agro-forestry, animal husbandry, dairying, fisheries, agricultural statistics, economics and marketing.

3.1.2 Important Organisations under the Ministry:

A. Indian Council of Agricultural Research (ICAR): ICAR is an autonomous organisation under the Department of Agricultural Research and Education (DARE), Ministry of Agriculture, Government of India. Formerly known as Imperial Council of Agricultural Research, it was established on July 16, 1929 as a registered society under the Societies Registration Act, 1860 in pursuance of the report of the Royal Commission on Agriculture. The ICAR has its headquarters in New Delhi.

ICAR is the apex body for co-ordinating, guiding and managing research and education in agriculture including horticulture, fisheries and animal sciences in the entire country. It is one of the largest national agricultural systems in the world.

ICAR has played a pioneering role in ushering Green Revolution and subsequent developments in agriculture in India through its research and technology development, thus making a visible impact on the national food and nutritional security. It has played a major role in promoting excellence in higher education in agriculture. It is engaged in cutting edge areas of science and technology development and its scientists are internationally acknowledged in their fields.

B. Commission for Agricultural Costs and Prices (CACP): The Agricultural Prices Commission was set up in January 1965 to advise the Government on price policy of major agricultural commodities with a view to evolving a balance and integrated price structure in the perspective of the overall needs of the economy and with due regard to the interests of the producer and the consumer. Since March 1985, the Commission has been known as Commission for Agricultural Costs and Prices (CACP).

CACP is composed of a Chairman, a Member Secretary, two official members and three non-official members. The non-official members are representatives of the farming community. They are usually persons with long field experience and active association with the farming community.

Assurance of a remunerative and stable price environment is considered very important for increasing agricultural production and productivity since the market place for agricultural produce tends to be inherently unstable, which often inflict undue losses on the growers, even when they adopt the best available technology package and produce efficiently. Towards this end, minimum support prices (MSP) for major agricultural products are fixed by the government, each year, after taking into account the recommendations of CACP.

C. National Seeds Corporation (NSC): Working since 1963, under the control of the Ministry of Agriculture of the Government of India. NSC undertakes production, processing and marketing of agricultural seeds. Its product range includes cereals, pulses, oilseeds, fodder, fibre and vegetable crops.

NSC pioneered the development of Indian seed industry on scientific lines with its involvement in the formulation of seed certification standards. Its seeds are evaluated for quality standards by independent seed certification agencies besides internal quality checks and laboratory tests in its own seed testing laboratories located in New Delhi, Secunderabad, Pune, Bhopal and Kolkata.

To meet the twin challenges of providing food and nutritional security to the people, agriculture production (especially of the foodgrains crops) has to be increased on sustained basis so as to achieve self-sufficiency in all major crops like cereals, pulses, oilseeds, fibres and fodder etc. For achieving the above objectives, seed is one of the critical inputs besides other inputs like fertilizers, irrigation, plant protection, farm practices etc. With the help of ICAR, NSC has been in the business of multiplication and production of seeds of all major crops. NSC is the single largest producer of certified seeds in the country in terms of quantity and third largest company in terms of turnover amongst all the seed producing companies including private sector companies.

NSC ensures to provide quality seeds of high yielding varieties and hybrids of all major cereal crops like paddy, wheat, maize, pulses, and oilseeds.

Apart from this main Ministry, there are at least 7 other Ministries of the Government of India which deal, in one way or the other, with subjects related to agriculture and allied activities. These are the following:

1. Ministry of Water Resources, River Development and Ganga Rejuvenation.
2. Ministry of Rural Development.
3. Ministry of Chemicals and Fertilizers.
4. Ministry of Food Processing Industries.
5. Ministry of Consumer Affairs, Food and Public Distribution.
6. Ministry of Panchayati Raj.
7. Ministry of Environment, Forest and Climate Change.

3.2 National Agriculture Policy (NAP), 2000

On July 28, 2000, Government of India announced a National Agriculture Policy to include this vital sector of the economy in the ambit of economic reforms. After the economic reforms in 1991-92 that removed the restrictive and protective licensing regime for industry, the policy focus turned to agriculture. There was the general impression that agriculture in India operated amidst a number of restraints and controls and that farmers did not receive the benefits of free trade as compared to other sectors of the economy. The main elements of NAP, 2000 were the following:

1. Private sector investment in agriculture would be encouraged, particularly in areas like agricultural research, human resource development, post-harvest management and marketing.
2. Catapulting agricultural growth to over 4 percent per annum by 2005.
3. Restrictions on the movement of agricultural commodities throughout the country would be progressively dismantled.
4. Appropriate measures would be adopted to ensure that agriculturists by and large, remain outside the regulatory and tax collection system.
5. Rural electrification would be given high priority as a prime mover for agricultural development.
6. Progressive institutionalisation of rural and farm credit would be continued for providing timely and adequate credit to farmers.

3.3 National Policy for Farmers, 2007

National Commission on Farmers (NCF) [Chairman: M.S. Swaminathan] was set up in 2004 to suggest an action plan for farmers and farm sector. The Commission submitted five Reports between December 2005 and October 2006. Main recommendations of the Commission included the following:

1. Asset reforms covering land, water, livestock and bio-resources.
2. Farmer-friendly support services covering extension, training and knowledge, connectivity, credit and insurance.
3. Assured and remunerative marketing.
4. Inputs and delivery services.
5. Curriculum reforms in the agriculture universities.
6. Bringing agriculture in the Concurrent List (List III) of the

Seventh Schedule of the Constitution.

7. Setting up of a National Food Security and Sovereignty Board.
8. Universalization of public distribution system (PDS).
9. Setting up of an Indian Trade Organization.
10. Converting Commission on Agriculture Costs and Prices into an autonomous statutory organization.
11. Minimum support prices (MSPs) for agricultural commodities to be at least 50 percent more than the cost of production.
12. Launching a Rural Non-farm Livelihood Initiative (RNFLI).

The NCF prepared, along with its final report, a draft National Policy for Farmers incorporating its main recommendations. Based on the draft prepared by the NCF and after consultations with State Governments and the Central Ministries concerned, Government of India approved the National Policy for Farmers, 2007. The primary focus of this policy is on 'farmer' defined holistically and not merely on agriculture. In that sense, it is much more comprehensive than an Agriculture Policy. The objective, *inter alia*, is to improve the economic viability of farming through substantially improving net income of farmers. There is emphasis on increased productivity, profitability, institutional support, and improvement of land, water and support services apart from provisions of appropriate price policy, risk mitigation measures and so on.

3.4 Recent Initiatives for Agricultural Development

3.4.1 Rashtriya Krishi Vikas Yojana (RKVY), 2007: Concerned by the slow growth in the agriculture and allied sectors, the National Development Council (NDC), in its meeting held on May 29, 2007 resolved that a special Additional Central Assistance Scheme. The NDC resolved that agricultural development strategies must be reoriented to meet the needs of farmers and called upon the Central and State governments to evolve a strategy to rejuvenate agriculture. The

NDC reaffirmed its commitment to achieve 4 percent annual growth in the agricultural sector during the Eleventh Five Year Plan (2007-12).

A. Basic Objectives of RKVY: RKVY aims at achieving 4 percent annual growth in the agriculture sector during the Eleventh Plan period by ensuring a holistic development of agriculture and allied sectors. The main objectives of the scheme are as under:

1. To incentivise the states so as to increase public investment in agriculture and allied sectors.
2. To provide flexibility and autonomy to states in the process of planning and executing agriculture and allied sector schemes.
3. To ensure the preparation of agriculture plans for the districts and the states based on agro-climatic conditions, availability of technology and natural resources.
4. To ensure that the local needs/crops/priorities are better reflected in the agricultural plans of the states.
5. To achieve the goal of reducing the yield gaps in important crops through focussed interventions.
6. To maximize returns to the farmers in agriculture and allied sectors.
7. To bring about quantifiable changes in the production and productivity of various components of agriculture and allied sectors by addressing them in a holistic manner.

B. Primary Strategic Relevance of the Scheme: RKVY Scheme is a State Plan scheme administered by the Union Ministry of Agriculture over and above its existing Centrally Sponsored Schemes. RKVY Scheme has bcen formulated with two strategic objectives in mind—first, to incentivize States to allocate more funds for agriculture and allied sectors and second, to focus States to generate additional growth in agriculture and allied sectors by better planning and undertaking appropriate growth oriented projects to achieve the goal. This is to be done by drawing up plans for their agriculture and allied sectors more comprehensively, by integrating livestock, poultry and fisheries reflecting needs/crops/priorities taking agro-climatic conditions, natural resource issues and technology into account. Funds under the scheme are provided to the States as 100 percent grant by the Central Government.

Allocation of funds to States is dependent on additional resources committed by States for agriculture and allied sectors in their state plans and growth projected and generated. There are no prescriptions about the projects, schemes and other programmes to be undertaken by States under RKVY. The Scheme provides complete flexibility to States to choose what is best suited in their conditions to generate growth so as to enable the country to achieve 4 percent growth in agriculture and allied sectors during the Eleventh Plan.

C. Areas of Focus under RKVY: An indicative list of focus areas has been provided for in the RKVY guidelines. Some of the areas covered are as under:

1. Integrated development of major food crops such as wheat, paddy, coarse cereals, minor millets, pulses and oilseeds.
2. Agricultural mechanization.
3. Activities related to enhancement of soil health.
4. Development of rain-fed farming systems.
5. Support to state seed farms.
6. Integrated pest management.
7. Strengthening of market infrastructure.
8. Extension services.
9. Animal husbandry and fisheries.
10. Promotion of horticulture.

D. Public-Private-Partnership for Integrated Agricultural Development (PPPIAD): To augment the current government efforts in agricultural development by leveraging the capabilities of the private sector, PPPIAD has been recently launched under RKVY. The scheme envisages facilitating large scale integrated projects, led by private sector players in the agriculture and allied sectors, with a view to aggregating farmers, and integrating the agriculture supply chain with financial assistance through RKVY.

The Government has approved continuation of the RKVY scheme during the Twelfth Five Year Plan (2012-17) whereby

RKVY funding will be routed into three components, viz. production growth, infrastructure and assets, and sub-schemes and flexi-fund. The proposed allocation for implementation of this scheme during 2015-16 was ₹ 18,000 crore. In view of the need to increase capital formation and get higher returns on investments, states are at liberty to spend up to 100 percent of total outlay in the infrastructure and asset creation component.

RKVY is a transformational jump in evolution of agricultural development schemes from variegated schematic approach followed so far through diverse but strait-jacketed schemes to a completely new approach in agriculture planning by allowing the States to plan their strategy and design appropriate schemes to implement that strategy with complete flexibility in scheme designs and autonomy in its implementation.

RKVY has imparted definite momentum to the agriculture sector. Regular activities starved of resources, promising strategies languishing for lack of support, and limited opportunities for experimentation and innovation, have found a new hope in RKVY. States are allocating more funds to agriculture to take up schemes of agriculture development. This is reflected in additional plan allocation to agriculture sector. There is a sense of hope and optimism. Agriculture, which had slid back, is making a comeback. RKVY has accelerated revival of agriculture and put it on growth path.

3.4.2 Macro Management of Agriculture (MMA) Scheme: Agriculture is a state subject. Hence, the primary role for increasing productivity and production of food grains and other agriculture crops is that of the State Governments. However, in order to supplement the efforts of the State Governments, a number of Centrally-sponsored and Central Sector Schemes are being implemented for enhancement of agricultural productivity and production for livelihood security of the farming community and food security in the country.

MMA Scheme was launched in 2000-01 by integrating 27 centrally sponsored schemes moving away from a programmatic to a macro management mode of assistance to the states in the form of work plans prepared by the states and implemented in a spirit of partnership with the states. The scheme was conceived to be a step to provide sufficient autonomy and initiative to state governments to develop programmes and activities as per their felt needs and priorities. The scheme replaced the schematic rigid approach by a work-plan-based approach in an interactive mode to supplement and complement states' efforts in the agriculture sector.

MMA scheme was a major step towards decentralization, allowing states the flexibility to choose suitable interventions from the various components in addition to their own efforts towards growth of the agriculture sector. Later, with the launch of the National Horticulture Mission in 2005-06, 10 components relating to horticulture were excluded from the MMA scheme. Thus, the MMA scheme comprises the following 17 components or sub-schemes, focusing on rice, wheat, coarse cereals, sugarcane, soil health, nutrient and pest management, farm mechanization and watershed development:

1. Integrated cereal development programmes in rice-based cropping system areas.
2. Integrated cereal development programmes in wheat-based cropping system areas.
3. Integrated cereal development programmes in coarse cereals based cropping system areas.
4. Special jute development programme.
5. Sustainable development of sugarcane based cropping system.
6. Balanced and integrated use of fertilizer.
7. Promotion of agricultural mechanization among small farmers.
8. National watershed development project for rain-fed areas.
9. Scheme for foundation and certified seed production of vegetable crops.
10. Soil conservation in catchments of river valley projects and flood prone rivers.
11. Reclamation and development of alkali soils.

12. State land use board.
13. Assistance to co-operatives of weaker sections.
14. Assistance to women co-operatives.
15. Non-overdue cover scheme.
16. Agriculture credit stabilization fund.
17. Special scheme for SC/ST.

A. Revised MMA Scheme: In the year 2008-09, the MMA scheme was revised to improve its efficacy in supplementing and complementing the efforts of the States towards enhancement of agricultural production and productivity. Role of the Scheme was redefined to avoid overlapping and duplication of efforts and to make it more relevant to the present agricultural scenario in the States to achieve the basic objectives of food security and improving the livelihoods of rural masses. Revised MMA scheme comprised 11 sub-schemes relating to crop production and natural resource management. Further, one sub-scheme relating to State Land Use Board (SLUB) was discontinued with effect from August 1, 2009. The revised MMA scheme now comprises 10 sub-schemes, which are as under:

1. Integrated cereal development programmes in rice-based cropping system areas.
2. Integrated cereal development programmes in wheat-based cropping system areas.
3. Integrated cereal development programmes in coarse cereals based cropping system areas.
4. Integrated development programme for pulses and oilseeds (new scheme included as one of the crop production programmes).
5. Sustainable development of sugarcane based cropping system.
6. Balanced and integrated use of fertilizers.
7. Promotion of agricultural mechanization among small farmers.
8. National watershed development project for rain-fed areas.
9. Soil conservation in catchments of river valley projects and flood-prone rivers.

10. Reclamation and development of alkali soils.

The salient features of the revised MMA Scheme are as follows:

1. Practice of allocating funds to States/UTs on historical basis has been replaced by a new allocation criteria based on gross cropped area and area under small and marginal holdings.
2. Assistance under MMA would be provided to the States/UTs as 100 percent grant.
3. Subsidy structure has been aligned to make subsidy pattern uniform under all the schemes implemented by the Department of Agriculture and Co-operation. Revised subsidy norms indicate the maximum permissible limit of assistance. States have freedom to retain existing norms, or increase them to a reasonable level provided that the same do not exceed the specified revised upper limits.
4. Two new components have been added namely: (a) Pulses and oilseeds crop production programmes for the areas not covered under the Integrated Scheme of Oilseeds, Pulses, Oil Palm and Maize (ISOPOM) and (b) "Reclamation of Acidic Soil" to the existing component of "Reclamation of Alkali Soil".
5. Ceiling for new Initiatives has been increased from existing 10 percent to 20 percent of the allocation.
6. At least 33 percent of the funds have to be earmarked for small, marginal and women farmers.
7. Active participation of the panchayati raj institutions (PRIs) of all tiers has to be ensured in the implementation of the revised MMA scheme including review, monitoring and evaluation at district/sub-district level.

3.4.3 Extending Green Revolution to the Eastern States: This programme envisages adoption of new seed varieties, farm machinery, integrated nutrient and pest management, and knowledge-based interventions developed for different agro-climatic zones. The programme is under implementation in Bihar, Chhattisgarh, Jharkhand, Eastern Uttar Pradesh, West Bengal and

Odisha. Recently, the state of Assam has also been included under this initiative.

3.4.4 Integrated Scheme of Oilseeds, Pulses, Oil Palm and Maize (ISOPOM): This scheme is being implemented in 14 major states for oilseeds and pulses, in 15 states for maize and in 9 states for the oil palm.

3.4.5 Support to State Extension Programmes for Extension Reforms: The objective of the Scheme is to make the extension system farmer-driven and farmer-accountable by way of new institutional arrangements for technology dissemination. 598 Agricultural Technology Management Agencies (ATMAs) have been established at district level to operationalize the extension reforms. The scheme was modified in 2010 to provide for the following activities:

1. Provision of specialist and functionary support at different levels.
2. Innovative support through a 'Farmer Friend' at village level.
3. Revision in ATMA Cafeteria.
4. Farmers' Advisory Committees at State, district and block levels.

3.4.6 National Project on Promotion of Organic Farming (NPOF): This is a continuing scheme from Tenth Five Year Plan (2002-07) with an outlay of ₹ 101 crore in the Eleventh Five Year Plan (2007-12). The revised mandate, effective from 2010-11, lays stress on technical capacity building, information generation and promotion of organic farming in the country. Major components include the following:

1. Financial assistance for setting up of fruits/vegetable market waste compost units and bio-fertilisers and bio-pesticides production units.
2. Technical capacity building and human resource development through trainings and research.
3. Development and regulation of quality control of organic inputs.
4. Biological assessment of soil health.
5. Launching and operationlisation of low cost certification

system known as Participatory Guarantee System (PGS).

6. Awareness creation and publicity for increasing adoption of organic farming in the country.

3.4.7 Policy Framework for Agricultural Extension (PFAE): The need for reforms in agricultural extension was explicitly raised in the National Agriculture Policy. To provide policy directives for extension reforms, PFAE was approved by the Ministry of Agriculture, Government of India, in March 2005. It is the main scheme to revamp agricultural extension across the country. It aims at providing a decentralized and demand driven extension system by way of new institutional arrangements for technology dissemination in the form of an Agricultural Technology Management Agency (ATMA) at district level.

The 5 major guiding elements of PFAE are as follows:

1. Reforming public sector extension.
2. Promoting private sector to effectively complement, supplement and wherever possible to substitute public extension.
3. Augmenting media and information technology support for extension.
4. Mainstreaming gender concerns in extension.
5. Capacity building/skill upgradation of farmers and extension functionaries.

The reforms enlisted above have been pilot-tested under Innovations in Technology Dissemination (ITD) component of World Bank-funded National Agricultural Technology Project (NATP) with effect from November 1998 in 7 states, viz. Andhra Pradesh, Bihar, Himachal Pradesh, Jharkhand, Maharashtra, Odisha and Punjab, covering 4 districts in each state. An autonomous institution—Agricultural Technology Management Agency (ATMA)—has been established in these project districts as a registered society representing various stakeholders, including farmers, in project planning and implementation. Monitoring and Evaluation (M&E) reports of ITD component brought out by Indian Institute of Management (IIM), Lucknow reveal that extension approaches of ATMA have proved very promising in execution of reforms envisaged in PFAE.

3.4.8 Agricultural Technology Management Agency (ATMA): ATMA is a district level body created under the ITD component of NATP for pilot testing agricultural extension reforms. This is an autonomous institution with participation of all the key stakeholders involved in agricultural activities for sustainable agricultural development. It has the flexibility to receive funds directly from Central and State Governments, membership fees, beneficiaries contribution etc. ATMA has the main responsibility of all the technology dissemination activities at the district level. It has linkages with all the line departments, research organizations, non-governmental organizations and agencies associated with agricultural development in the district with a substantial representation of organizations of farmers. Research and extension units within the district, such as department of agriculture, horticulture, animal husbandry, fisheries, sericulture, marketing etc. are constituent members.

3.4.8 Organic Farming: To increase crop yields in rain-fed areas, which account for nearly 55 percent of the country's arable land, organic farming is being promoted. Towards this end, the Government has launched two important schemes. First, the *Parmparagat Krishi Vikas Yojana* which will bring 5 lakh acres under organic farming over a three year period. Second, the Government has launched a value chain based organic farming scheme called Organic *Value Chain Development in North East Region*. The emphasis is on value addition so that organic produce grown in these parts find domestic and export markets. A total provision of ₹ 412 crore was made for these schemes in the 2016-17 Budget.

4

Agricultural Inputs and Services

Against the backdrop of burgeoning demand of population for foodgrains, degrading natural resource base, emerging concerns of climate change and other challenges, the Government has focused on mobilizing higher investment in agriculture, bridging yield gaps that exist across the states/regions, timely and adequate supply of quality inputs, and providing adequate support services to the farmers to make agriculture a remunerative vocation on a sustainable basis. Increasing agricultural production with limited natural resources in a sustainable manner for ensuring food and nutritional security and providing income security to farmers are the major challenges before the Government. Accelerating the rate of growth of agricultural production must be seen as central to a more inclusive growth.

4.1 Seeds, Insecticides, Farm Machines and Agricultural Research

4.1.1 Seeds: One of the most outstanding achievements of modern agriculture is the production of improved varieties of seed for different crops. The cultivator is generally well aware of the importance of using good seed. Good cultivators are known to preserve their own seed. Certain varieties of seed have spread by themselves without special departmental efforts, and if improved seed is not making such headway as it should, the cause must be sought in some defect in the seed or elsewhere than in the apathy of the cultivators.

The National Seeds Policy, 2002 provides the framework for growth of the seed sector. It seeks to provide the farmers with a wide range of superior quality seed varieties and planting materials.

To meet India's obligation under TRIPS Agreement of the

WTO, Protection of Plant Varieties and Farmers' Rights Act, 2001 was enacted to protect the intellectual property rights of plant breeders and to stimulate investments in R&D for the development of new plant varieties. The Act involves setting up of an Authority for implementing the provisions of the Act. Necessary rules and regulations under the Act have been notified.

Protection of Plant Varieties and Farmers' Rights (PPV&FR) Authority was established in November 2005 and has the mandate to implement the PPV&FR Act, 2001, with a view to establish an effective system for protection of plant varieties, rights of farmers' and plant breeders and encourage development of new varieties of plants. Accordingly, the Authority is taking steps for putting in place an intellectual property rights regime in agriculture for development of new varieties of plants and protection of rights of farmers' and breeders in the country.

In response to the changes that have taken place in the seed sector, the existing Seeds Act, 1966 is proposed to be replaced by a suitable legislation. Therefore, the Government introduced the Seeds Bill in the Rajya Sabha in December 2004. The Bill provides for compulsory registration of seeds on the basis of their performance, deregulation/decontrol of seed industry/processing units and imposition of more stringent penalties to check the sale of spurious seeds. The process of getting the Bill passed by Parliament is underway.

4.1.2 Plants Protection and Insecticides: Plant protection is an important component of crop production programme. Plant protection activities encompass plant quarantine, regulation of pesticides, activities aimed at minimizing crop losses due to pests (including locust control in desert areas), and training and capacity building in plant protection.

The triple alliance of pests, pathogens and weeds is the cause of substantial crop losses every year.

Plant Quarantine (Regulations of Import into India) Order, 2003, made operational from January 1, 2004, contains adequate provisions to prevent the introduction of exotic pests, diseases and weeds into India.

Insecticides Act, 1968 regulates the import, manufacture, sale, transportation, distribution and use of insecticides with a view to prevent risk to humans or animals, and for matters connected therewith.

Pesticides Management Bill, 2008 is intended to replace the Insecticides Act, 1968 to provide for a more effective regulatory framework for the introduction and use of pesticides in the country. It was introduced in the Parliament (Rajya Sabha) on October 21, 2008. The Parliamentary Standing Committee on Agriculture placed its report on the Bill in the Parliament on February 18, 2009. The recommendations of the Standing Committee were examined, and taking these into account, the official amendments to the Bill were finalized for consideration and passing in Rajya Sabha. The process of passing the Bill is underway.

4.1.3 Agricultural Implements and Machines: India is a labour-surplus economy and there is a great deal of disguised unemployment in the agricultural sector. It is true that by using modern agricultural machines productivity of land can be raised. However, there are fears that such an approach will displace labour, adding to the already huge army of unemployed and underemployed people. Whatever may be the arguments for and against mechanization of India agriculture, the fact of the matter remains that farmers in many parts of the country are adopting modern mechanical devices to boost their farm productivity.

It is generally accepted that by using improved implements a larger area can be covered in the same time, and the timely performance of agricultural operations results in reduction of costs as well as better yields.

4.1.4 Agricultural Research: Agricultural research is of a continuing nature. New knowledge has to be gained, and fresh problems tackled. The role of universities in promoting agricultural research is a question which needs attention. Although universities are eminently suited for such research, especially of the more fundamental type, they have not taken it up to any significant extent in the past, owing perhaps to lack of funds and other causes. Limitations in the way of the universities to take an appropriate part in agricultural research should be removed and the universities encouraged to make their contribution to research. This will benefit the universities also by bringing their scientific staffs into direct contact with real problems which are in urgent need of solution for the betterment of the vast majority of rural people.

Department of Agricultural Research and Education (DARE) of the Ministry of Agriculture, Government of India has an extensive network comprising 97 central institutes, 6 national bureaux, 25 project directorates, 18 national research centres and 89 all-India co-ordinated research projects. It also supports research and education in 53 state agriculture universities, 5 deemed universities and 1 Central agriculture university. Over the years, co-ordinated efforts have helped the country improve varieties of sugarcane, rice, wheat, maize, sorghum, groundnut, mustard etc., considering the ecological variations with respect to each crop.

There is a need to associate representatives of progressive cultivators, traders and processors with the drawing up of annual research programmes and their evaluation.

4.2 Fertilizers Use and Subsidy Policy

Successive Five Year Plans have laid stress on self-sufficiency and self-reliance in foodgrains production and concerted efforts in this direction have resulted in substantial increase in agriculture production and productivity. In India's success in agriculture sector—not only in terms of meeting total requirement of foodgrains but also generating exportable surpluses—the significant role played by chemical fertilizers is well recognized and established. Keeping in view the vital role played by chemical fertilizers in the success of India's green revolution and consequent self-reliance in foodgrains production, the Government of India has been consistently pursuing policies conducive to increased availability and consumption of fertilizers in the country.

4.2.1 Production, Consumption and Imports of Fertilizers: The consumption of fertilizers has been steadily increasing over the years. A great deal of variability is observed in fertilizer consumption between the States. Amongst States in the plains per hectare consumption is highest in Punjab, Haryana, Andhra Pradesh and Tamil Nadu. It is lowest in Madhya Pradesh and Rajasthan. *Kharif* crops account for nearly one-third of the total fertilizer consumption, whereas the *rabi* crops accounted for a much larger share. This has now changed. Consumption is more evenly spread between the two sowing seasons, reflecting perhaps more assured water availability in *kharif* season at all India level.

Of all the fertilizers, urea dominates the sector (Table 4.1). It is the most produced (86 percent), the most consumed (74 percent share), and the most imported (52 percent). It also faces the most government intervention. Urea is the most physically controlled fertiliser, with 50 percent under the Fertiliser Ministry's movement control order compared with 20 percent for DAP and MOP. It also receives the largest subsidies, in outlay terms (accounting for nearly 70 percent of total fertilizer subsidy) and as proportion of actual cost of production (75 percent per kg., compared with about 35 percent for DAP and MOP)

4.2.2 Fertilizer Pricing Policy, Control and Subsidy: Government interventions in urea and DAP/MOP differ not just in scale, but also in kind. DAP and MOP producers and importers receive a nutrient based subsidy (NBS) based on a formula that determines the amount of N, P and K in a given amount of fertiliser. Per kg. subsidies on DAP and MOP fertiliser are hence fixed—they do not vary with market prices. Imports of DAP and MOP are also not controlled. The prices farmers face are thus deregulated market prices adjusted by fixed nutrient subsidy. Government involvement in DAP and MOP is limited to paying producers and importers a fixed nutrient based subsidy which works out to be roughly 35 percent of the cost of production (Table 4.2).

Table 4.1: Production, Consumption and Imports of Fertilizers (2014-15)

	Production		Consumption		Imports	
	Volume (000' MT)	Value ₹ crore	Volume (000' MT)	Value ₹ crore	Volume (000' MT)	Value ₹ crore
DAP	3,445	12,471	7,626	27,606	3,853	13,948
MOP	...	...	2,853	7,418	4,197	10,912
Urea	22,593	43,830	30,610	59,383	8,749	16,973

Source: Government of India, *Economic Survey*, 2015-16, Volume 1, Chapter 9, Table 9.1.

Table 4.2: Basic Fertiliser Price Facts (2014-15)

	Domestic Subsidised Price (₹/50 kg.)	International Price (₹/50 kg.)	Subsidy (₹/50 kg.)	Import Restriction	Percent of Volume that is under Movement Control
DAP	1,200	1,810	618	None	20
MOP	800	1,300	465	None	20
Urea	270	970	807	Canalised	50

Note: Numbers in bold are prices fixed by the Government. The others are market prices.
Source: Government of India, *Economic Survey*, 2015-16, Volume 1, Chapter 9, Table 9.1.

The case of urea is very different. The government intervenes in the sector in five ways:

1. It sets a controlled maximum retail price (MRP) at which urea must be sold to farmers. This price is currently ₹ 5,360 per metric tonne—approximately ₹ 268 per 50 kg. bag—less than one-third the current imported price (₹ 18,600 per tonne).
2. It provides a subsidy to 30 domestic producers which is firm-specific on a cost-plus basis, meaning that more inefficient producers get larger subsidies. [1]
3. It provides a subsidy to importers which is consignment-specific.

4. Imports are canalised—only three agencies are allowed to import urea into India.
5. About half of the movement of fertilizers is directed—that is, the government tells manufacturers and importers as to how much to import and where to sell their urea.

Thus, nearly all stakeholders—consumers, producers, importers, distributors—are controlled. These distortions feed upon each other, and together create an environment that leads to a series of adverse outcomes which are described below.

4.2.3 Black Market in Fertilizers: Urea is only subsidised for agricultural uses. Subsidy like this violates what is called the *One Product-One Price* principle—the intuition that products which are essentially the same should be charged essentially the same price, else there will be incentives to divert the subsidised commodity from eligible to ineligible consumers. The 75 percent subsidy on agricultural urea creates a large price wedge which feeds a thriving black market, diverting urea to industry [2] and possibly across the border to Bangladesh and Nepal. [3] According to one estimate, 41 percent of urea is diverted to industry or smuggled across borders. It is estimated that about 51 percent of Indian farmers buy urea at above MRP. In the three eastern states bordering Bangladesh, 100 percent of farmers had to buy urea at above MRP in the black market. Similarly, in Uttar Pradesh, which borders Nepal, 67 percent of farmers had to buy urea in the black market at above the stipulated MRP. [4]

These black market prices are, on average, about 61 percent higher than stipulated prices (i.e. MRP plus local taxes), indicating that black marketing imposes significant pecuniary costs on farmers—in addition to creating uncertainty of supply.

Black market effects are aggravated by a further regulation—canalisation. Only three firms [State Trading Corporation of India (STC), Metals and Minerals Trading Corporation of India (MMTC) and India Potash Limited (IPL)] are allowed to import urea into India, and the canalisers are also instructed when to import, what quantities to import, and in which districts to sell their goods. Every season the Fertiliser Department estimates how much imports are required by forecasting domestic supply and demand. Forecasting fertiliser demand is a difficult business, and misestimates—especially shortages—are difficult to correct because the system to procure imports is time consuming. The entire process—from the time the Fertiliser Department decides to import to the time urea reaches consumer centres—takes about 60-70 days. These delays can exacerbate shortages, and are particularly costly during the peak demand period when timely availability of urea is essential for proper plant growth. Farmers are thus pushed to purchase in the black market.

The black market hurts small and marginal farmers more than large farmers since a higher percentage of them are forced to buy urea from the black market. This regressive nature is characteristic of black market rationing and happens because large farmers are typically better connected and therefore able to secure scarce subsidized urea.

4.2.4 Soil Health Card Scheme: Through this scheme—announced by the Finance Minister in his 2016-17 Budget Speech—farmers get information about nutrient level of the soil and can make judicious use of fertilizers. The target is to cover all 14 crore farm holdings by March 2017. Union Budget 2016-17 provided ₹ 368 crore for the National Project on Soil Health and Fertility. Besides, 2,000 model retail outlets of fertilizer companies will be provided with soil and seed testing facilities during the next three years. Fertilizer companies will also co-market city compost which increases the efficacy of chemical fertilizer. A policy for conversion of city waste into compost has also been approved by the Government under the *Swachh Bharat Abhiyan.*

4.3 Water Resources and Irrigation Programmes/Schemes

With 2.3 percent of the world's total area and 17.5 percent of the world's population, India has only 4 percent of the total fresh water available in the world. This clearly indicates the need for development, conservation and optimum use of water resources.

By and large, rainfall, surface and ground water resources have been sufficient in providing adequate water to the Indian population. Rise in demand and development pressures are changing the characteristics of water in India. Erosion in the watershed due to the fast growing development and poor land management practices is increasing siltation and changing stream hydraulics. Ground water reserves are becoming more and more depleted as surface water sources have become too polluted for human use.

Two-thirds of India's farm production comes from one-third of its land which is irrigated. The rest is from rain-fed areas that employ large populations. In order to meet the increasing demand for food and farm employment, India has to increase the area under irrigation, and enhance productivity in both irrigated and rain-fed areas.

In India, water and electricity for irrigation are subsidized for political reasons. This leads to wasteful flood irrigation rather than adoption of more optimal practices such as sprinkler and drip irrigation. Cropping patterns and farming practices also do not necessarily encourage the judicious use of water. Conservative estimates indicate that the same quantity of irrigation water used presently can irrigate double the current area with optimized irrigation and farming practices.

With limited revenues and budgetary support, the state engineering departments are unable to operate and maintain the efficiency of irrigation systems, leading to increasing deterioration of the structures and systems over time. Consequently, there are further water losses due to breaches and seepage, resulting in water logging and salinity. Water quality is further affected due to the overuse of chemical fertilizers and pesticides. The environmental challenges of water resources development and management in India are expected to manifest themselves more explicitly and rapidly in the coming years.

4.4 Agricultural Credit and Rural Co-operatives

Rural indebtedness is noted as a major reason for the spurt in farmer suicides during recent times across a number of states. In most, if not all, such cases, the economic status of the suicide victim was very poor, being small and marginal farmers. After the Green Revolution, agricultural activities have become cash-based individual enterprises requiring high investment in modern inputs and wage labour. This is evident from the list of states with high incidence of farmer suicides, which are not necessarily backward or predominantly agrarian or with low income. Increased liberalization and globalisation have in fact led to a shift in cropping pattern from staple crops to cash crops like oilseeds and cotton, requiring high investment in modern inputs and wage labour, and increasing credit needs but when the prices decline farmers have no means to supplement their incomes.

4.4.1 Rural Co-operatives: Short-term rural co-operatives provide crop and other working capital loans to farmers and rural artisans primarily for short-term purposes. These credit institutions have a three-tier federal structure: (a) at the apex of the system is a state co-operative bank (SCB) in each State; (b) at the middle (or district) level, there are central co-operative banks (CCBs) also known as district co-operative banks; and (c) at the lowest (or village) level are the primary agricultural credit societies (PACS). The smaller States and Union Territories (UTs) have a two-tier structure with SCBs directly meeting the credit requirements of PACS.

Long-term rural co-operatives provide typically medium and long-term loans for making investments in agriculture, rural industries and, in the recent period, housing.

4.5 Micro Finance, Self-help Groups (SHGs) and NABARD

The micro finance initiative of NABARD, i.e. SHG-Bank Linkage Programme has passed through various phases over the last one and half decades, *viz.* pilot testing during 1992 to 1995, mainstreaming during 1996 to 1998 and expansion from 1998 onwards.

Micro credit has emerged as a visible credit channel to the poor as their access to conventional credit channels is constrained by the requirement of collateral and high transaction cost. Micro finance is routed through self-help groups (SHGs). Over the years, SHG-Bank Linkage Programme—which includes commercial banks, regional rural banks and co-operative banks—has emerged as the major micro finance programme in the country. The focus under SHG-Bank Linkage Programme is largely on those rural poor who have no sustainable access to the formal banking system. The target groups, therefore, broadly comprise small and marginal farmers, agricultural and non-agricultural labourers, artisans and craftsmen and other poor engaged in small businesses like vending, and hawking.

The programme has been providing the rural poor access to the formal banking system and has achieved several milestones in terms of gender sensitisation, empowerment and poverty alleviation. The programme provides thrift linked credit support to the members of SHGs. While the programme directly benefits the members, it also helps banks in reducing their transaction costs as well as risk in delivering small loans.

The programme has now assumed the form of a micro finance movement in many parts of the country and has started making inroads in the resource poor regions of the country as well.

4.5.1 Kisan Credit Cards (KCCs): KCC is a pioneering credit delivery innovation—launched by NABARD in August 1998—for providing adequate and timely credit to farmers under single window, with flexible and simplified procedure, adopting whole farm approach, including the short-term credit, medium term and long term credit needs of the borrowers for agriculture and allied activities and a reasonable component for consumption needs.

Beneficiaries covered under the Scheme are issued with a credit card and a pass book or a credit card-cum-passbook incorporating the name, address, particulars of land holding, borrowing limit, validity period, a passport size photograph of holder etc., which may serve both as an identity card and facilitate recording of transactions on an ongoing basis.

Borrower is required to produce the card-cum-passbook whenever he/she operates the account.

4.6 Agricultural Marketing and Trade

Marketing is the last link in the chain of production process. An efficient marketing system which ensures reasonable return to the producers is essential to induce them to produce more. Disposal of the produce after harvest and the return obtained have a significant effect on production and on the welfare of the cultivator.

Sale of agricultural produce involves a number of functions such as assembling, storing, grading, standardising, transporting and financing the produce and negotiating sale. Some of these operations may be performed by the farmer, but storage and sale of a commodity and finding finance for purchase, call for specialised knowledge and adequate resources which the individual cultivator does not possess.

The Government has been playing an important role in developing the agricultural marketing system in the country. Department of Agriculture Cooperation and Farmers Welfare in the Ministry of Agriculture and Farmers Welfare, Government of India, has 3 organizations dealing with marketing under its administrative control, namely Directorate of Marketing and Inspection (DMI) Faridabad, Chaudhary Charan Singh National Institute of Agricultural Marketing (NIAM), Jaipur and Small Farmers Agri-business Consortium (SFAC), New Delhi.

Ministry of Agriculture, Government of India launched the ICT-based Central sector scheme of agricultural marketing information network (AGMARKNET) in March 2000 to link important agricultural produce markets spread all over the country and the State Agriculture Marketing Boards and Directorates. The project is being executed with the technical support of National Informatics Centre (NIC).

In order to facilitate wider market access to farm produce and better price discovery through value addition, the scheme is additionally disseminating information on market requirements in terms of quality, packing, standards, sanitary and phyto-sanitary conditions etc.

4.7 Agricultural Insurance

Agriculture insurance is not restricted to crop insurance only, although it is one of the most important and major constituents of agriculture insurance. Agriculture insurance is much wider in scope and content and includes insurance of seed, cattle, horticulture, plantations, forestry, sericulture, aquaculture, poultry, viniculture and all such activities which are allied to agriculture. In its wider connotation, it should cover all operations commencing from sowing of seeds to marketing of final products which are connected to agriculture. It will also include all the capital equipments used during different stages of agricultural operations such as tractors, threshing machines, drought animals, pumpsets, processing plants etc. From this angle, agriculture insurance can be treated as synonymous with rural insurance.

4.7.1 National Agriculture Insurance Scheme (NAIS): Introduced from *rabi* 1999-2000 season, the main objective of the scheme is to protect the farmers against crop losses suffered on account of natural calamities, such as, drought, flood, hailstorm, cyclone, pests and diseases.

Due to some limitations/shortcomings in the existing NAIS, Modified NAIS was approved for implementation on pilot basis in 50 districts from *rabi* 2010-11 season in the country. Administrative approval and operational guidelines for the scheme were issued on September 17, 2010 and September 28, 2010 respectively.

The major improvements made in MNAIS are the following.

1. Actuarial premium with subsidy in premium at different rates, i.e. 40 percent to 75 percent depending upon the slab is provided to farmers.
2. All claims liability would be on the insurer.
3. Unit area of insurance has been reduced to village panchayat level for major crops.

4. Indemnity has been provided for prevented/sowing/planting risk and for post-harvest losses due to cyclone.
5. On account payment up to 25 percent advance of likely claims can be made as immediate relief.
6. More proficient basis for calculation of threshold yield, minimum indemnity level of 70 percent instead of 60 percent and private sector insurers with adequate infrastructure have been allowed.
7. Only upfront premium subsidy is shared by the Central and State Governments on 50:50 basis and the claims are the liability of the insurance companies.
8. Uniform seasonality discipline for loanee and non-loanee farmers.
9. The scheme is compulsory for loanee farmers and voluntary for non-loanee farmers.
10. Private sector insurers with adequate infrastructure and experience would be allowed in the implementation of MNAIS.
11. NAIS would be withdrawn for those area(s)/crop(s) of the districts in which MNAIS is implemented.

4.7.2 Agriculture Insurance Corporation: Union Budget 2002-03 proposed setting up of a separate Corporation for Agriculture Insurance to be promoted by the existing public sector general insurance companies. A task force was constituted to oversee the setting up of the Agriculture Insurance Corporation. It was decided by the Task Force that the new company will be named as 'Agriculture Insurance Company of India Ltd.' and will be registered under the Companies Act, 1956 with the capital participation from General Insurance Corporation of India (GIC), four public sector general insurance companies, viz. National Insurance Company Ltd., New India Assurance Company Ltd., Oriental Insurance Company Ltd. and United India Insurance Company Ltd. and NABARD.

The promoters' subscription to the paid-up capital will be 35 percent by GIC, 30 percent by NABARD and 8.75 percent each by the four public sector general insurance companies. The authorised capital of the new organization will be ₹ 1,500 crore, while the initial paid-up capital will be ₹ 200 crore. National Agriculture Insurance Scheme (NAIS) shall be transferred to the new organization and shall form the core of business to begin with. Transition to actuarial regime will be made over a period of time. The new organization will, in due course, cover other allied rural/agricultural risks in addition to crop insurance.

The Registrar of Companies (Delhi and Haryana) approved the name of the new company as Agriculture Insurance Company of India Ltd. The new company was incorporated under the Companies Act, 1956 on 20.12.2002.

4.8 Information Technology (IT) in Agriculture

See chapter 6 of this book.

4.9 Agricultural Exports and Imports

4.9.1 Agricultural Exports: Marine products, rice, wheat, sugar, oil meals, tea, coffee, cashew and spices are the prominent products of India's agriculture exports. Meat and meat preparations, fruits and vegetables and processed fruits and vegetables have recently shown strong growth. Despite the advantage of diverse agro-climatic conditions, enabling production of a great variety of products in various seasons, India's exports potential has not yet been adequately addressed. Main reasons for this are the following.

1. Poor export infrastructure.
2. Low level of agriculture product grading.
3. Lack of quality control.
4. Poor branding and packaging.

Infrastructure specific to agriculture exports such as storage, and fast track inland and mechanical port handling facilities are also limiting factors.

In the Export-Import (EXIM) Policy 2002-07, Government announced the proposal to set up agriculture export zones (AEZs) for the purpose of developing and sourcing raw materials and their processing/packaging leading to final exports. The underlying objective is to promote agricultural exports from the country and ensure remunerative returns to the farming community in a sustained manner.

The concept essentially embodies a cluster approach of identifying the potential products and the geographical region in which such products are grown and adoption of an end-to-end approach of integration of the entire process, right from the stage of production to consumption.

Under the scheme, the State Governments identify products with export potential which have comparative advantage in local production. State Government evolve a comprehensive package of services provided by all State Government agencies, State agriculture universities and all institutions and agencies of the Central Government for intensive delivery in these zones. Corporate entities with proven credentials are also encouraged to sponsor new AEZs or take over already notified AEZs or part of such zones for boosting agriculture exports from the zones.

4.9.2 Agricultural Imports: In recent years, edible oil, accounting for nearly 60 to 65 percent of the value of total agriculture imports, has become the single largest import item. Raw cashew, nuts (almonds from US) and pulses are among the other dominant agriculture imports. Of late, the share of agriculture imports in total imports of the country has hovered around 4 to 5 percent.

Lifting of quantitative restrictions on imports since April 2000 has resulted in import of a number of agriculture products which include fruits, juices, ketchups, meat products etc. Monitoring of 300 sensitive product imports has so far revealed that such imports are limited and, in the aggregate, constitute a small proportion of total agriculture imports. Contrary to concerns in some circles that liberalization of imports—resulting from the lifting of quantitative restrictions on agriculture products—would lead to surge of agriculture imports affecting adversely the Indian farmers, the value of agriculture imports in aggregate terms is quite low. India has considerable flexibility to counter flooding of the Indian market by cheap agriculture imports through imposition of tariffs (bound rate) under WTO. WTO permissible tariff rates are reasonably high as compared to actual rates. This should provide a fair level of protection. Countervailing duties can also be imposed to counter questionable subsidies given to agriculture products by the exporting countries apart from having the option of acting under safeguard provisions to counter surge of imports.

To conclude, while there have been efforts—such as those to promote institutional credit to rural areas, improved access to inputs, subsidies on fertilisers and electricity, minimum support price etc.—these have not been fully successful in protecting the interest of the farmers in general, and small/marginal farmers in particular. Small/marginal farmers have inadequate access to: (a) information, (b) agencies promoting technological change, (c) co-operative networks and related organisations, and (d) plethora of governmental interventions. This is significant since, in any case, these farmers are less well placed to take advantage of the markets.

Endnotes

1. The Government introduced the new urea policy in 2015 covering the period 2015-16 to 2018-19. Under this policy gas-based urea plants are placed in three categories based on energy norms. In the first 3 years, energy norms are plant specific but from 2018-19 plants are expected to adopt group/category specific energy norms.
2. Urea is used as one of the ingredients in chemical industry, explosives, automobile systems, laboratories, medical uses, flavour enhancing additive in cigarettes and others.
3. A 50 kg. bag of urea in India costs around ₹ 268 while it is Tk 800 (₹ 685) in Bangladesh and NPR 996 (₹ 622) in Nepal.
4. Government of India, *Economic Survey*, 2015-16, Volume 1, Chapter 9, paras 9.11 and 9.12.

5

Diversification of Indian Agriculture

Plantation, horticulture, animal husbandry, dairy farming and fisheries sectors play an important role in the national economy and in the socio-economic development of the country. These sectors also play a significant role in supplementing family incomes and generating gainful employment in the rural sector, particularly among the landless labourers, small and marginal farmers and women, besides providing cheap nutritional food to millions of people. Livestock are the best insurance against the vagaries of nature like drought, famine and other natural calamities.

The Government has identified horticultural crops as a means of diversification for making agriculture more profitable through efficient land use, optimum utilization of natural resources (soil, water and environment) and creating skilled employment for rural masses, especially women folk.

5.1 Need for Diversification of Indian Agriculture

India's future agricultural development will require much faster crop diversification in view of changes in consumption pattern. There is growing preference for milk and milk products, meat, poultry, fish, fruits and vegetables. Areas like horticulture and floriculture also hold promise as they have higher export potential.

According to Reserve Bank of India (RBI), "A contributing factor to below-potential performance of agriculture is the failure to sufficiently diversify the cropping pattern. The minimum support price (MSP) policy has distorted the relative prices between rice and wheat, on the one hand, and other food and non-food crops, on the other, giving rise to a distorted cropping pattern. It has contributed to a steep rise in the ratio of procurement to production over the years. The higher increase in MSPs of rice and wheat relative to prices of other agricultural commodities has contributed to an incentive structure that favours production of rice and wheat at the cost of other crops. The policy has contributed to a burgeoning stock—far in excess of food security requirements, adding to carrying costs and locked-in bank credit, which could have been otherwise deployed for funding productive activities". [1]

Emphasising the need for diversification of Indian agriculture, the Tenth Five Year Plan (2002-07), observed, "Finally, the true potential of Indian agriculture can be realised only when there is diversification of agricultural products, both geographically and over time. The food and nutritional requirements of the people for leading healthy lives demand a wider range of food products than are presently consumed on the average. For such diversification to gain momentum, the requisite science and technology inputs will have to be provided along with appropriate supportive price policies. Most of the non-grain food products are, however, perishable in nature. In order to encourage the diversification through minimum wastage, considerable attention will be required to focus on post-harvest technologies and marketing infrastructure. It would also require a reconsideration of the various rules and regulations that govern agricultural trade, which frequently act against the interests of the farmers and distort their incentive structure". [2]

5.2 Plantation Sector

The Government of India has taken a series of steps to promote tea, coffee, rubber, bamboo and coconut plantations.

5.2.1 Tea Plantation

1. Replacement of the central excise duty payable on tea by an additional duty of excise of ₹ 1 per kilogram for creating a separate fund for long-term development and modernisation of the tea plantation sector.
2. Implementation of a credit relief package announced by

RBI to help the tea industry.

3. Introduction of a price sharing formula for equitable sharing of the sale proceeds between the bought leaf factories and small tea growers.
4. Implementation of IT-based information dissemination plan for the tea industry, including conversion of manual auction centres into electronic auction centres.

5.2.2 Coffee Plantation

1. Re-phasement/restructuring of loans taken by the coffee growers from commercial banks.
2. Providing interest relief to coffee growers on their working capital loans taken from financial institutions.
3. Undertaking campaigns to promote domestic consumption of coffee.
4. Reduction of import duty on specified machinery for coffee sector to 5 percent to enable the industry to improve the quality and productivity of coffee for making it globally competitive.
5. Convincing the commercial banks to provide working capital loans to coffee growers at reduced interest rates.

5.2.3 Rubber Plantation

1. A number of plan schemes are being implemented. These schemes provide for suitable financial/technical assistance to the growers, processors, exporters etc. for increasing production of natural rubber through expansion of area, enhancing productivity, improving the quality of produce to achieve competitiveness in the global markets and promoting agricultural and technological research in the interest of the industry.
2. In the context of boosting export of natural rubber and establishing India as regular exporter of this commodity, Government is implementing Export Promotion of Natural Rubber Scheme since 2001-02. The scheme inter alia provides for financial assistance to the exporters of natural rubber for quality upgradation, certification, transportation etc.

3. To regulate the import of inferior rubber coming into the country, which was passing as standard rubber, Government has enforced conformity with BIS standards on imported rubber also, as in the case of domestic rubber.
4. Implementation of a Price Stabilization Fund Scheme with a corpus of ₹ 500 crore for the benefit of the growers of tea, coffee, rubber and tobacco.

It is noteworthy that amounts deposited in Tea Development Account or Coffee Development Account or Rubber Development Account or 40 percent of profits and gains from business of growing and manufacturing tea, or coffee or rubber are deductible as admissible expenses under Section 33AB of the Indian Income Tax Act, 1961.

5.2.4 National Bamboo Mission (NBM): Bamboo is the fastest growing plant on this planet. Bamboos are characterized by woody, mostly hollow culms with internodes and branches at the culms nodes. India is the second richest country in terms of bamboo genetic diversity with a total of 136 species under 75 genera. It encompasses about 8.96 million hectares of forest area, which is equivalent to 12.8 percent of the total forest cover of the country.

In order to harness the potential of bamboo crop, Ministry of Agriculture, Government of India, launched a Centrally-sponsored scheme called National Bamboo Mission in 2006-07. The thrust of NBM is on area-based, regionally-differentiated strategy for both forest and non-forest areas.

5.2.5 Coconut Development Board (CDB): CDB is a statutory body set up by the Government of India for integrated development of coconut cultivation and industry in the country. Coconut provides food and livelihood security to more than 10 million people across 18 States and 3 UTs in the country. There are 5 million coconut holdings in the country and the average size of these holdings is less than 1 hectare.

The thrust areas of CDB are the following:

1. Production and distribution of quality planting material.
2. Expansion of area under coconut cultivation especially in

potential and non-traditional areas.

3. Improving the productivity of coconut in major coconut producing states.
4. Developing technology in post-harvest processing and marketing activities.
5. Integrated control of major pests and diseases.
6. Product diversification.
7. By-product utilization of coconut for value addition.

5.3 Horticultural Crops

Soon after Independence in 1947, India's agricultural policy was to achieve self-sufficiency in foodgrains production to tide over the imbalances in food supplies caused by the Partition of the country in that year. However, over the years, horticulture has emerged as an indispensable part of agriculture, offering a wide range of choices to the farmers for crop diversification. It also provides ample opportunities for sustaining large number of agro-industries which generate substantial employment opportunities. The sector encompasses a wide range of crops, namely fruit crops, vegetables crops, potato and tuber crops, ornamental crops, medicinal and aromatic crops, and spices. New introductions like mushroom, and bee-keeping have further expanded the scope of horticulture.

There is a realization that growing horticulture crops is now an option to improve livelihood security, enhance employment generation, attain food and nutritional security and increase income through value addition. Over the years, there has been a significant improvement in the production of horticulture crops.

Recent efforts have been rewarding in terms of increased production and productivity and availability of a much larger volume of horticultural produce. India has emerged as the largest producer of coconut, arecanut, cashewnut, ginger, turmeric, black pepper and the second largest producer of fruits and vegetables. Among the new crops, kiwi, olive crops and oil palm have been successfully introduced for commercial cultivation in the country.

Efforts are on to encourage private investment in hi-tech horticulture with micro-propagation, protected cultivation, drip irrigation, and integrated nutrient and pest management besides making use of latest post-harvest technology, particularly in the case of perishable commodities. Resultantly, horticulture crop production has begun to move from rural confines to commercial ventures and has attracted young entrepreneurs, since it has proved to be intellectually satisfying and economically rewarding.

5.3.1 National Horticulture Mission (NHM): NHM was launched on April 1, 2005. It ensures an end-to-end approach having backward and forward linkages covering research, production, post-harvest management, processing and marketing, under one umbrella, in an integrated manner.

The objective of NHM is to promote holistic growth of the horticulture sector through area-based, regionally-differentiated strategies. The major programmes under NHM include: (a) supply of quality planting material through the establishment of nurseries and tissue culture units, (b) production and productivity improvement programmes through area expansion and rejuvenation, (c) technology promotion, (d) technology dissemination, (e) human resource development, (f) creation of infrastructure for post-harvest management and (g) marketing in consonance with the comparative advantages of each state/region and their diverse agro-climatic conditions.

All States and UTs are covered under NHM except the states that are covered under the Horticulture Mission for North East and Himalayan States (HMNEH). NHM endeavours for the holistic development of horticulture sector duly ensuring forward and backward linkages by adopting cluster approach, with the active participation of all stake-holders. Presently, 371 districts in 18 States and 3 Union Territories are covered under NHM.

Apart from the States and Union Territories, 13 National Level Agencies (NLAs) have been included for providing support for the developmental efforts which require inputs at the National Level.

Horticulture sector has grown significantly over the years. India has maintained leadership in the production of many commodities like mango, banana, coconut, arecanut, cashew, ginger, turmeric and black pepper.

5.3.2 Mission for Integrated Development of Horticulture (MIDH): With effect from 2014-15, the Mission for Integrated Development of Horticulture (MIDH) has been operationalized by bringing all ongoing schemes on horticulture under a single umbrella. Production and distribution of quality planting material, productivity improvement measures through protected cultivation, use of micro irrigation, adoption of integrated pest management and integrated nutrient management along with creation of infrastructure for post-harvest management and marketing are focus areas of the MIDH.

5.4 Animal Husbandry

Livestock plays an important role in Indian economy and is an important sub-sector of Indian agriculture. Livestock provides stability to family income especially in the arid and semi-arid regions of the country and is an insurance against the vagaries of nature due to drought, famine and other natural calamities. Major part of the livestock population is concentrated in the marginal and small size of holdings.

Livestock sector not only provides essential proteins and nutritious human diet through milk, eggs, meat etc., but also plays an important role in utilization of non-edible agricultural by products. Livestock also provides raw material/by products such as hides and skins, blood, bone, fat etc.

Market opportunities have opened up for the livestock sector following the economic liberalization. However, the sector's ability to capitalize on new market opportunity is constrained by the availability and quality of support services which at present, are mainly provided by the Government. Moreover, these services are not available at the doorsteps of the producers. There is a need to restructure service delivery mechanism to become conducive to the requirement of the rural livestock producers. Lack of credit for livestock production has been a major problem. Public sector lending is very low. The strategy should be to correct these distortions and ensure timely availability of inputs and services including credit to livestock farmers.

The National Policy for Farmers announced by the Government in 2007 also addressed the problems related to livestock activities and government's response to them. It stated, "Livestock, including poultry, is also one of the important sources of livelihood, contributing about one fourth of the agricultural GDP. These activities engage women in much larger proportion. The ownership of livestock is much more egalitarian since poor farmer families mostly own cattle, buffalo, sheep and goats. The major constraints experienced by farmers relate to breed, fodder, feed, healthcare and remunerative prices for their produce. There is a need to address these issues through an appropriate strategy. Further, to enhance the income of livestock owners, agri-clinics operated by veterinary and farm science graduates would be encouraged to improve productivity and overall efficiency of livestock. At the same time, crop-livestock mixed farming systems would be promoted, apart from encouraging production of organic manures and bio-fertilizers. Livestock insurance would also be revamped and made accessible to all farmers.

For poultry farming, the following steps would be taken:

- Quarantine and testing facilities for imported birds and vaccines at all ports of entry would be established and strengthened, since such safeguards are necessary for the health and survival of the poultry industry and for the protection of life and livelihood.
- Testing for safety and efficacy of imported poultry vaccines before they are allowed to be marketed, as is done in the case of human vaccines, would be made compulsory.
- Poultry rearing would be recognised as an agricultural activity and appropriate support would be provided to backyard poultry farmers to promote clusters or small

holders' poultry estates". [3]

Government has been operating various central livestock organizations and allied institutions for production and distribution of superior germplasm to the State Governments for cross-breeding and genetic upgradation of the stocks. Besides, it is implementing various central sector and Centrally-sponsored schemes for the development of requisite infrastructure and supplementing efforts of the State Governments in achieving accelerated growth of animal husbandry sector.

5.5 Dairy Farming

The Indian dairy sector has acquired substantial growth momentum in recent years. This has ensured sustained growth in the availability of milk and milk products for the growing population. Dairying has become an important secondary source of income for millions of rural families and has assumed the most important role in providing employment and income-generating opportunities. Government of India is making efforts to increase the productivity of milch animals and thus increase the per capita availability of milk. Milk production and marketing system in India is unique. Most of the milk is produced by small, marginal farmers and landless labourers.

The efforts in the dairy sector are concentrated on promotion of dairy activities mainly in non-operation flood areas with emphasis on building up cooperative infrastructure, revitalization of sick dairy cooperative federations and creation of infrastructure in the States for production of quality milk and milk products.

5.5.1 National Dairy Development Board (NDDB): It was set up in 1965 in Anand (Gujarat) to promote, plan and organise programmes for the development of dairy and other agriculture based and allied industries along cooperative lines, and also to provide assistance in the implementation of such programmes. In 1987, the Parliament declared NDDB as a statutory body corporate and an institution of national importance under the NDDB Act.

5.5.2 National Dairy Plan: National Dairy Plan is a strategic plan prepared by NDDB with an estimated outlay of ₹ 17,371 crore to achieve a target of 180 million tonnes of milk production annually by 2021-22. Milk production is expected to grow at 4 percent with an annual incremental output of 5 million tonnes in the next 15 years. Districts will be categorized into 324 high potential districts for intensive development and 282 low potential districts for further expansion of the sector. Under this plan the Government is contemplating to enhance milk production in major milk producing areas, strengthen and expand infrastructure to produce, process and market milk through the existing and new institutional structures. The plan envisages breed improvement through artificial insemination and through natural service, setting up plants to augment cattle feed, by-pass protein and mineral mixture and expanding/strengthening milk processing infrastructure. The plan also proposes to bring 65 percent of the surplus milk produced under organized sector for procurement as against the present 30 percent. The cooperative and private sector would continue to have 50:50 share.

5.5.3 Milk Production: India continues to be the largest producer of milk in the world. Several measures have been initiated by the Government to increase the productivity of livestock. Table 5.1 shows the production and per capita availability of milk in recent years.

With the increase in milk production, quality standards prevalent today in milk production, milk collection and processing need improvement. The microbiological quality of milk is poor due to lack of knowledge about clean milk production and lack of post-milking chilling facilities in the villages. To compete in international market for export of milk and milk products, it has become necessary to produce the dairy products of international standards.

Export of milk powders (including skimmed milk powder, whole milk powder, dairy whitener and infant milk foods) was prohibited with effect from February 18, 2011 to augment the availability of liquid milk and stabilize the prices of milk and milk products.

Table 5.1: Production and Per Capita Availability of Milk in India: 1990-91 to 2015-16

Year	Production (million tonnes)	Per Capita Availability (grams/day)
1990-91	53.9	176
2000-01	80.6	220
2010-11	121.8	281
2011-12	127.9	290
2012-13	132.4	299
2013-14	137.7	307
2014-15	146.3	322
2015-16	155.5	337

Source: Department of Animal Husbandry, Dairying and Fisheries, Ministry of Agriculture and Farmers Welfare, Government of India.

5.5.4 Poultry Farming: Poultry development has been a household activity in India. The poultry sector has emerged from entirely unorganized farming practice to commercial production system with State-of-the-art technological interventions. Poultry sector, besides providing direct or indirect employment to people, is also a potent tool for subsidiary income generation for many landless and marginal farmers. It also provides nutritional security especially to the rural poor.

A. Central Poultry Development Organizations (CPDO): CPDOs, located at 4 regions, viz. Chandigarh, Bhubaneswar, Mumbai and Bangaluru, have been playing a pivotal role in the implementation of the policies of the Government with respect to poultry. The mandate of these organizations has been reoriented to focus on improved indigenous birds, which lay on an average 180-200 eggs per annum and have vastly improved feed conversion ratio in terms of feed consumption and weight gain. Training is also imparted in these CPDOs to the farmers to upgrade their technical skills. Besides, CPDOs, Bangaluru is also imparting trainers' training to in-service personnel from within the country as well as overseas. Diversification with species other than chicken like ducks, turkey, guinea fowl, Japanese quail and emu is also undertaken.

The Central Poultry Performance Testing Centre (CPPTC), located in Gurgaon is entrusted with responsibility of testing the performance of layer and broiler varieties. CPPTC gives valuable information relating to different genetic stock available in the country.

B. Poultry Venture Capital Fund: The main objective of the scheme is to encourage entrepreneurship skills of individuals in various poultry activities. Under it, various poultry activities like establishing poultry breeding farms, feed godown, feed analytical laboratories, marketing of poultry products have been funded as interest free loans.

5.6 Fisheries

Fisheries sector occupies a very important place in the socio-economic development of India. It has been recognised as a powerful income and employment generator as it stimulates growth of a number of subsidiary industries and is a source of cheap and nutritious food, besides being a foreign exchange earner. At the same time it is an instrument of livelihood for a large section of economically backward population of the country. Table 5.2 shows the production of fish in recent years.

Fisheries is a State subject as per Entry 21 of List II (State List) of the Seventh Schedule of the Constitution of India and as such the primary responsibility for its development rests with the State Governments. The major thrust in fisheries development has been on optimizing production and productivity, augmenting export of marine products, generating employment and improving welfare of fishermen and their socio-economic status.

5.6.1 Marine Fishing Policy, 2004:

A. Policy Objectives: Marine Fishing Policy, 2004 has the following objectives:

1. To augment marine fish production of the country up to

the sustainable level in a responsible manner so as to boost export of sea food from the country and also to increase per capita fish protein intake of the masses.

2. To ensure socio-economic security of the artisan fishermen whose livelihood solely depends on this vocation.
3. To ensure sustainable development of marine fisheries with due concern for ecological integrity and bio-diversity.

Table 5.2: Production of Fish in India: 1950-51 to 2013-14

Year	Fish Production ('000 tonnes)		
	Marine	Inland	Total
1950-51	534	218	752
1960-61	880	280	1,160
1970-71	1,086	670	1,756
1980-81	1,555	887	2,442
1990-91	2,300	1,536	3,836
2000-01	2,811	2,845	5,656
2010-11	3,250	4,981	8,231
2011-12	3,372	5,294	8,666
2012-13	3,321	5,719	9,040
2013-14	3,443	6,136	9,579

Source: Department of Animal Husbandry, Dairying and Fisheries, *Handbook on Fisheries Statistics, 2014*, Table A-1, page 5 (excerpted), Ministry of Agriculture and Farmers Welfare, Government of India.

B. Main Provisions of the Policy: These are as under:

1. **Marine Fisheries Resources:** The policy underscores the need for a departure from the open access concept in the territorial waters besides putting in place stringent management regimes. Promoting exploitation in the deep sea and oceanic waters would be another approach for reducing fishing pressure in the traditional fishing areas.
2. **Harvesting of Marine Fish Resources:** The policy advocates protection, consideration and encouragement of subsistence level fishermen and technology transfer to small scale sector and infrastructure support to industrial sector. There would be exclusive areas in terms of depth

and (or) distance earmarked for non-mechanised (non-motorised) traditional craft. An area beyond this would be demarcated for mechanized and motorised craft.

3. **Post-harvest Operations:** Total utilisation of harvested fish for food and non-food uses would be the central theme. Efforts would be made to fully comply with international requirements in post harvest care of catch so as to achieve highest standards in food safety. It would also be the concern of the Government to ensure that the post-harvest losses are minimized.
4. **Resource Management:** Exploitation of living resources within 50 metres depth zone is showing symptoms of depletion and in certain belts in the onshore waters, it tends to cross optimum sustainable levels. The policy therefore advocates a stringent fishery management system to be in place.
5. **Fishermen Welfare:** Fishing is the sole livelihood for about 10 lakh fishermen households along the coastline and this policy attaches top priority to ensuring their social security and economic well being.
6. **Environmental Aspects:** The effect of environmental factors on the health of living resources needs increased attention in tune with the international awareness on the issue. Health hazards due to consumption of fish harvested from contaminated water is also becoming a matter of great concern in many parts of the world. The agencies responsible for legislation relating to environmental pollution would be urged to implement them more stringently so that the impact of pollution on fisheries can be minimized.
7. **Infrastructure Development for Marine Fisheries:** Development of infrastructure for marine fisheries is of vital importance and should have an integrated approach. The facilities would inter alia include jetties, landing centres, provision for fuel, water, ice, repairs to vessels and gear. The concept of hygienic post harvest handling of fish would also be woven into the project.
8. **Legislative Support:** An enabling legal framework is an

essential pre-requisite for proper management and control of fisheries sector. As at present, the subject of fisheries is in the State list of the Indian Constitution, management and control of coastal fisheries is vested with the maritime States and Union Tèrritories. At the same time the Union Government carries out management and control of the fishing activities beyond territorial limits in the EEZ.

9. **Policy for Development of Fisheries in the Union Territories of Lakshadweep, and Andaman and Nicobar Islands:** The waters around these two Island Groups are rich in fish resource, which are currently exploited far below the exploitable limits. Fisheries, capture, post harvest operations and marketing, is still an important means of livelihood for the inhabitants of these islands. It is, therefore considered relevant to have the policy initiatives in respect of the two UTs.

5.6.2 National Policy for Farmers (2007) on Fisheries: It proposed various steps to promote modern aquaculture practices and value addition. It observed, "Both coastal and inland fisheries provide employment and livelihood to millions of families. There is considerable scope for improving the income of fishermen families on an environmentally sustainable basis by encouraging scientific fish rearing, harvesting and processing. In the area of public policy, there is a need for well-planned aquarian reforms in order to provide landless labour families access to village ponds and other water bodies in the public domain for aquaculture.

The NFDB has been established by the Government of India to bring major activities relating to fisheries and aquaculture for focused attention and professional management. The guiding principles for the NFDB would be ecology, economics, gender equity, employment generation and advising the state governments to facilitate rational and equitable allocation of public water bodies and reservoirs for practicing modern aquaculture.

Following steps will be taken to promote modern aquaculture practices and value addition:

1. *Fish for All* training and capacity-building centres to impart training to fisher families and fisher-women in all

aspects of the capture/culture/consumption chain, quality literacy for hygienic handling and other aspects.

2. Provision of small dredgers for ensuring the efficiency of fishlanding centres.
3. Centralised services to support the decentralised capture and culture fisheries sectors.
4. Inland aquaculture, including the culture of ornamental fish and air breathing fish, by providing necessary space in ponds and reservoirs.
5. Artificial coral reefs to compensate for the loss of natural coral reefs to revive the fish catch.
6. Raising bio-shields comprising Mangroves, Casuarina, Salicornia, Aatriplex and other halophytic plants, to safeguard the lives and livelihoods of coastal fisher and farm families in the event of cyclonic storms and seawater inundation during calamities like tsunamis.

A dynamic policy for the management and economic use of the Exclusive Economic Zone (EEZ) for a variety of economic activities, including fisheries, will be evolved and put in place with the assistance of NFDB". [4]

The main challenges facing fisheries development in the country include development of sustainable technologies for fin and shell fish culture, fish seed certification, yield optimization, infrastructure for harvest and post-harvest operations, landing and berthing facilities for fishing vessels and uniform registration of fishing vessels.

Endnotes

1. Reserve Bank of India, *Report on Currency and Finance,* 2001-02, p. VIII-2.
2. Government of India, Planning Commission, *Tenth Five Year Plan* (2002-07), Volume I, p. 15.
3. Government of India, Ministry of Agriculture, Department of Agriculture and Co-operation, *National Policy for Farmers*, 2007, p. 6.
4. Ibid., p. 7.

6

Information Technology (IT) for Agriculture and Rural Development

The face of the Indian agriculture can be transformed by a well conceived deployment of information technology (IT). The potential of IT as yet remains untapped and urgent measures are required to derive maximum benefit. The key players involved in this process such as industry, government and educational institutions and research centres are required to make contributions in this endeavour. The initiative to develop necessary IT-based agricultural services need to be developed immediately.

Various sectors of the Indian economy such as industry, finance, insurance, communications and transport have adopted information technology in a big way. However, agricultural sector of the economy is lagging behind in utilizing IT services. Some efforts have been made in this regard but they are by no means adequate. The rapid strides that the country has registered in the IT field will remain incomplete unless IT is fully utilised to ensure more efficient and productive Indian agriculture. Practically there is no area in agriculture in which IT has no role to play. The immense scale and diversity of Indian agriculture provides the ultimate challenge to the potential of information technology.

6.1 Need for IT-based Services to Farmers

India has emerged over the last decade as the most preferred destination for outsourcing of IT services. The vibrant IT industry is contributing immensely by providing information about latest technology and international business practices. Various sectors of the Indian economy such as industry, finance, insurance, communications and transport have adopted information technology in a big way. However, agricultural sector of the economy is lagging behind in utilizing IT services. Some efforts have been made in this regard but they are by no means adequate. The rapid strides that the country has registered in the IT field will remain incomplete unless IT is fully utilised to ensure more efficient and productive Indian agriculture. Practically there is no area in agriculture in which IT has no role to play. The immense scale and diversity of Indian agriculture provides the ultimate challenge to the potential of information technology.

The adoption of IT services in agriculture depends on the main functionaries involved in Indian agriculture. These functionaries can make a big contribution to the growth of agriculture with the assistance of IT. For this purpose, the following functionaries can be considered: (a) farmers, (b) industries providing inputs to agriculture, (c) industries dealing with agricultural output, (d) central and state governments and (e) NGOs working for the benefit of farmers and agricultural universities and research centres.

Indian farmers, for whose welfare a huge government machinery is devoted, still suffer from the absence of right information at the required time. The farmers require timely information on weather conditions, sowing time, availability of inputs including credit, expert advice on maintaining crops in healthy conditions, information on markets and on all other areas of interest to them.

In spite of the best efforts and expenditure, the conventional apparatus has not been able to deliver the goods satisfactorily. Herein lies the role of IT which can efficiently address the concerns of farmers stationed at even remote locations. Low literacy levels, cost of computers, poor communication infrastructure make it impossible for individual farmers, particularly small farmers, to directly adopt IT. This calls for institutional efforts to provide IT-based services to farmers.

In order to keep pace with the state-of-the-art technologies, National Informatics Centre (NIC) has been conducting various training programmes on IT application on a regular basis from time to time for the user organisations of agriculture sector. Agricultural Informatics Division of NIC has taken up various initiatives in bringing IT-led development which includes Web-enabled applications, GIS-based applications, multimedia applications, database applications and E-governance and training etc.

6.2 Rural Portal of Ministry of Rural Development (MoRD)

MoRD has developed a number of applications to automate the processes of information generation and strengthening E-governance. Efforts have also been made to develop national level ICT solutions for some important activities like the land records computerization, MIS for Mahatma Gandhi National Rural Employment Guarantee Act (MGNREGA) and, online monitoring of schemes like Rural Bazaar, RuralSoft.

Rural Portal provides a gateway to around 150 websites. It provides details of schemes of the Ministry, their physical and financial status, release position, sanction orders etc. Apart from this, news related to Ministry is also uploaded daily onto the site. Circulars of public interest, information regarding events, tenders/notices, e-mail are also uploaded regularly onto the site. Online SARAS Mela is available on the website to web showcase the products made by rural artisans for wide publicity and to create national/international market for their products. Applications have been developed to monitor on-line the Monthly Progress Reports of schemes of the Ministry.

NIC-DRD informatics cell has designed and developed the software for the household survey BPL Census, 2002. The software was designed in such a way that it uniquely identifies a family and all the members of the family at national level. It also assigns a unique number to all panchayats which are the executing agencies/service providers for most of the schemes of MoRD. The family and the persons whose information is captured in the software are the beneficiary/service receiver for most of the schemes of MoRD and are uniquely identified.

6.3 National Rural Employment Guarantee Act Software Package (NREGASoft)

MoRD and NIC commenced the preparation of appropriate E-governance solution to strengthen NREGA in October 2005 and when the scheme was launched in February 2006, the NREGASoft was also launched across the country. The software is available to all stakeholders online through www.NREGA.nic.in and also could be downloaded for off-line working. The package is Unicode-enabled and supports local languages. The training to use the software has been organized in States.

NREGAsoft is web-based software prepared to capture all the activities under NREGA at National/State/District/Block and Panchayat level. Using this portal each stakeholder can input information and access his/her own information through this portal. NREGAsoft captures Registration of workers, work demanded, number of days of employment for whole family, funds transferred/utilized and number of works undertaken under the scheme. Various stake holders of the project are the following:

1. Citizens.
2. Gram panchayats, block panchayats zilla panchayats.
3. Workers.
4. Programme officers.
5. District programme co-ordinators.
6. Implementing agencies other then PRIs.
7. State RD Departments.
8. Ministry of Rural Development and administrators in Government of India.

6.3.1 Various Modules of the Software: These are the following:

A. Beneficiary Management Module: It captures registration, demand for work, work allocation and muster rolls on which a person worked, the software has the provision of payment of wages through bank/post office as it captures the bank/post office account number, bank/post office name, branch name for all the person who demanded job and their account number are shown in muster roll against their name and calculate unemployment allowance, if any and also keep tracks of number of days of employment of a family.

B. Fund Management Module: It captures the funds transferred from MoRD/States to districts and then to programme officers/panchayats and expenditure incurred by various implementing agencies on labour, material and contingency. Hence, it keeps track of each and every paisa spent under the scheme.

C. Works Management Module: It captures information about the various works under taken under the scheme at various level. It facilitates online approval of projects and keeps track of time taken for approval of project. Each project is provided a unique ID and status of work is maintained in the system.

D. Grievance Redressal System: It allows a worker/citizen to lodge complaint and trace the subsequent response.

E. Staffing Position Module: It captures name, telephone numbers etc. of all the officials, planning and implementing agencies from gram panchayat to MoRD involved in NREGA, thus strengthening communication and co-ordination among them.

F. Alerts: The software also gives alerts to implementing agencies about various irregularities, important activities, messages for funds to be received by the agencies.

G. Gram Panchayat Accounting System: NREGA has put a lot of responsibility on gram panchayats as registration, demand for work and allocation of work can be done only by gram panchayats. Software assists gram panchayats as follows:

1. It keeps track of 100 days of the employment to a family.
2. It ensures that a worker should not work on two worksites simultaneously.
3. The software keeps track of the fund released from the MoRD/States to the districts and then from districts to blocks/gram panchayats so it helps in reconciliation of accounts.
4. It provides status of available funds in the accounts at panchayats, blocks and districts levels.

6.4 IFFCO-ISRO Co-operation

IFFCO has initiated IT-based services for farmers and cooperative societies. It has taken up a project in association with Indian Space Research Organisation (ISRO) to utilise satellite based remote sensing data and Geographical Information Systems (GIS). Developed countries have been utilising precision farming with the help of IT tools for a long time. While this will take a long time for our country due to small holdings, it is to be noted that GIS has an invaluable role to play even in the existing conditions. Remote sensing and GIS information can provide warnings on evolving crop stresses, crop vigour etc.

The IFFCO-ISRO GIS project extends support for efficient and timely availability of IFFCO's fertiliser to farmers though better logistics and efficient operations. Based on the experience gained from this project, more intensive services based on GIS are envisaged for the entire country. In addition to the GIS-based services, effort is being made to create databases that contain information of interest to the farmers. These include recommendation on package of practices for major cereals, pulses, horticulture, floriculture and animal husbandry etc. Information on various inputs such as seeds, fertilisers, credit is provided. An important service envisaged is to provide access to the nearest expert in case of stress or any other problem witnessed in the crops. Facilities are sought to be provided to encourage and share farm experiences by forging various crop forums. Many of the agricultural extension services are also proposed to be made online using multimedia facilities.

In order to encourage farmers to obtain best possible price, information regarding prices of various crops prevailing in approachable markets (mandies) is also being provided. Other areas of interest to farmers such as distance education, location specific news etc. are also planned.

6.5 Cyber Dhabas

To take IT to the door steps of the farmers, it is proposed that a large number of access points called cyber dhabas are setup.

These cyber dhabas should be provided with a PC and a modem with telephone connection to connect to the databases. The farmers can take the assistance of the operator of cyber dhabas for a nominal charge. The major bottleneck in spreading e-culture to rural areas is related to connectivity i.e. ensuring that the access points can get connected to the databases which are in selected locations. Since dialup lines are very slow, other viable options are required to be explored. Unfortunately, the alternatives are expensive and may not be feasible. One silver lining is that several private operators are connecting important cities with fibre optic which provides a very reliable and fast access. Since these will pass through rural areas, it is possible to explore the possibility of tapping this potential by laying the last mile connectivity. Once this is done, substantial segment of rural India can access the IT-based services.

6.6 E-Choupal

E-choupal offers farmers the information, products and services they need to enhance productivity, improve farm-gate price realisation, and cut transaction costs. Farmers can access the latest local and global information on weather, scientific farming practices, as well as market prices at the village itself through this web portal-all in Hindi. E-choupal also facilitates the supply of high quality farm inputs as well as the purchase of commodities at the farm.

Given the literacy and infrastructure constraints at the village level, this model is designed to provide physical service support through a choupal sanchalak, himself a lead farmer, who acts as the interface between the system and the farmers. The contents of this site in their entirety are made available only to the registered sanchalaks.

6.7 Kisan Call Centres (KCCs)

The scheme was launched on January 21, 2004 to provide agricultural information to the farming community through toll free telephone lines. A country wide common eleven digit number '1800-180-1551' has been allocated for KCC. The replies to the queries of the farming community are being given in 22 local languages. Calls are attended from 6.00 am to 10.00 pm on all 7 days of the week. In order to make farmers aware of this facility, audio and video spots on Kisan Call Centres are being broadcast telecast through All India Radio/ Doordarshan and private television channels. Kisan Knowledge Management system (KKMS) to provide correct, consistent and quick replies to the queries of farmers is being developed for each State/Union Territory.

6.8 E-Panchayat

As per the World Bank, "E-Government refers to the use by government agencies of information technologies (such as Wide Area Networks, the Internet, and mobile computing) that have the ability to transform relations with citizens, businesses, and other arms of government". Government of India, with an intention to transform the governance landscape by ensuring participation of citizens in policy making and providing ease of access to information to the citizens, introduced the National e-Governance Plan (NeGP) in 2006. The vision of the NeGP was to "Make all Government services accessible to the common man in his locality, through common service delivery outlets and ensure efficiency, transparency and reliability of such services at affordable costs to realise the basic needs of the common man".

E-Panchayat is one of the Mission Mode Project (MMP), currently being implemented with a vision to empower and transform rural India.

As a first step towards formulating the project, the Ministry of Panchayati Raj constituted an Expert Group in June, 2007 under the Chairmanship of Dr. B.K. Gairola, Director General, NIC, Government of India. The Expert Group was entrusted with the task of assessing the IT Programmes of Ministry of Panchayati Raj and recommending cost effective solutions along with the cost implications. Adopting a consultative approach, the

Committee interacted with the States/UTs to assess the existing status of computerization up to the Gram Panchayat level, including the initiatives undertaken by the State Governments.

In order to understand the ground realities, the Committee conducted field visits to some of the Gram Panchayats in the selected rural areas where some IT initiatives had been undertaken. Inputs from eminent experts in the public and private sector were also taken into account as part of the consultative process. In essence, it found that while some computerization efforts had already been made at Panchayat level by States like Gujarat, West Bengal, Karnataka, Kerala, Andhra Pradesh and Goa, these attempts were limited as they were driven by short term goals and were unable to completely transform Panchayats due to lack of a holistic perspective. It was felt that a more comprehensive approach was required to make a cognizable impact on the functioning of the Panchayats for the benefit of the citizens. These recommendations formed the basis for the conceptualization of e-panchayat MMP.

The e-panchayat project holds great promise for the rural masses as it aims to transform the panchayati raj institutions (PRIs) into symbols of modernity, transparency and efficiency. This is a one of its kind nationwide IT initiative introduced by Ministry of Panchayati Raj that endeavours to ensure people's participation in programme decision making, implementation and delivery. The project aims to automate the functioning of the 2.45 lakh Panchayats in the country. The project addresses all aspects of Panchayats' functioning including planning, monitoring, implementation, budgeting, accounting, social audit and delivery of citizen services like issue of certificates, licenses etc.

Subsequently, e-panchayat scheme was subsumed by Rajiv Gandhi Panchayat Sashaktikaran Abhiyan (RGPSA).

6.9 National e-Governance Plan in Agriculture (NeGP-A)

The underlying vision behind this project is to "create an environment conducive for raising farm productivity and income to global levels through provision of relevant information and services to the stakeholders". The initial phase of the project was envisaged to identity the key elements that need to be focused in agriculture and allied sectors. The next phase focused on detailed strategy, road map and guidelines for implementation of e-governance in agriculture at both Central and State levels. There are various IT initiatives and schemes undertaken or implemented by DAC which are aimed at providing information to the farmers on various activities in the agriculture value chain. These initiatives need to be integrated so that farmers may be able to make proper and timely use of the available information. Such information is intended to be provided to farmers through various channels including common service centres, internet kiosks and through SMSs.

6.10 Other IT Services to Agricultural Sector

6.10.1 LAN at Ministry of Agriculture: A high speed Local Area Network was established in the Ministry of Agriculture spread over various buildings viz. Krishi Bhawan (~500 nodes), Shastri Bhawan (~200 nodes), Krishi Anusandhan Bhawan (~100 nodes) etc. In addition, Agricultural Informatics Division has extended its full support (round the clock operation) to the Ministry of Agriculture at the time of super Cyclone in Orissa and Gujarat Earthquake. Video Conferencing facilities were used extensively from the Krishi Bhawan studio to Orissa and Gujarat on continuous basis.

6.10.2 Plant Protection Informatics and Communication Network (PPIN): The PPIN envisages to link the Directorate of Plant Protection Quarantine and Storage (DPPQS), Faridabad, National Plant Protection Training Institute, Hyderabad, CIMPS, LCC, Central Pesticides Testing Laboratories, and State Pesticides Testing Laboratories and to disseminate information related to plant protection and pesticides. As a part of project, the computerization of the CIB/RC of DPPQS has been taken up by NIC.

6.10.3 Agricultural Marketing Information Network (AGMARKNET): NIC has taken up an ambitious project "Agricultural Marketing Information Network (AGMARKNET)" on turnkey basis for the Directorate of Marketing and Inspection (DMI), Department of Agriculture and Cooperation, Ministry of Agriculture. The project aims at improving the prevailing agricultural marketing information system by minimising the gap between generation and dissemination of market information. The major components of AGMARKNET are the following: (a) establishment of computing facilities and networking, (b) development of human resource, (c) information transmission, (d) development of database and (e) portal on market information. NIC has tied up with Bharat Sanchar Nigam Ltd. (BSNL) to provide internet facilities at the AGMARKNET nodes.

6.10.4 Strengthening of Informatics in the Offices and Field Units of the Department of Agriculture and Cooperation (DAC)–DACNET: To promote e-Governance in Agriculture at the Centre and to provide support to States/UTs for the same, DAC is implementing this Central Sector Scheme. The scheme has the following components:

1. IT apparatus at DAC Headquarters, field offices and Directorates.
2. Development of Agricultural Informatics and Communication.
3. Strengthening of IT Apparatus in Agriculture and Cooperation in the States and Union Territories (AGRISNET).
4. Kisan Call Centres.

6.10.5 MIS Support to Food Processing Industries: To cater to the needs of the Department, NIC has developed various information systems viz. FPO and licensing monitoring, Plan scheme monitoring, industrial approvals, processed food products, FPO online status, industrial entrepreneur's memoranda query information, country profile and international cooperation etc.

6.10.6 Agricultural Extension Information System Network: VISTARNET: Research, education, extension, and training are considered as four pillars of sustainable agriculture.

Generation and transfer of technology have become very crucial the world over. As a step towards making technology reach the small holders (resource-poor-farmers), efforts are being made to establish VISTARNET–NICNET based Agricultural Extension Information System Network, in India, linking extension functionaries at Central, State, and District level. The required funds for implementing VISTARNET will be provided through the National Agricultural Technology Project (NATP). As a part of VISTARNET, Informatics Development for the Directorate of Extension has been taken up by NIC.

6.10.7 Indian Agriculture On-line: NIC has submitted an IT-Plan for the agriculture sector with the objective of establishing NICNET based Agricultural Informatics and Communication Network **(AGRISNET)** to facilitate higher and sustainable agriculture productivity and also putting **Indian Agriculture on-line** in the Country.

6.10.8 Infrastructural Facilities and Services Provided by NIC to the Ministry of Agriculture: These are the following:

1. Intranet/Internet.
2. Telecommuting programme.
3. Video conferencing.
4. Information kiosk.
5. In-house training facilities.
6. Website design and development.
7. Web-enabled applications.
8. Information bulletin.
9. Intranet applications.
10. Agriculture portal.
11. NICNET based Public Information and Facilitation Centre.

6.10.9 Animal Production and Health Information Network (APHNET): APHNET envisages building up of reliable databases and network based information systems for all activities of the animal husbandry and dairying sector at district, state and national level, using NICNET facilities. In view of importance of making technology reach the small holders through IT, the plan also suggests to establish APHNET nodes at about

42,000 veterinary polyclinics, hospitals, and dispensaries and veterinary aid centres for strengthening animal disease surveillance and advisory system in the country. As a part of APHNET, National Project on Rinderpest Eradication (NPRE) which aims at capturing animal disease related information from various State Animal Husbandry Departments has been entrusted to NIC.

6.10.10 Agricultural Research Information System Network (ARISNET): The ARISNET, a close user group of institutions in National Agricultural Research System of India (NARS) on NICNET, links ICAR Institutions and their Regional Research Stations, Central Agricultural University, State Agricultural Universities and their colleges, Krishi Vigyan Kendras, Zonal Research Centres and Project implementing centres with the ICAR Headquarters. ARISNET has become an integral part of agricultural research, extension and education process.

6.10.11 Market Information System for Horticulture: This project has been taken up by NIC on a turnkey basis. As part of the project, NICNET based internet/intranet facilities have been established at National Horticulture Board (NHB), Gurgaon. Computing facilities have been created at 33 market centres of the Board located all over the country. NIC has developed and implemented the necessary software for evolving a comprehensive database of the prices and arrivals of fruits and vegetables being received by NHB headquarters from 33 market centres on a daily basis. This information is being used by the Ministry of Agriculture, its related agencies and markets through National Bulletin on fruits and vegetables.

6.10.12 Integrated Fertilizer Management Information System (FERMIS): The Department of Fertilizers (DOF) in collaboration with National Informatics Centre (NIC) has introduced computer-based methods for decision support with the major objective to evolve an evaluation system which ensures a uniform system of Planning and control mechanism with signalling system to highlight deviations from desired performance indicators by plants/organisations for all the public sector fertilizer enterprises. Thus, an Integrated Fertilizer Management Information System (IFMIS) worth ₹ 1.99 crore has been executed through NIC and various IT-based systems developed covering planning, movement, imports, handling-payments, project monitoring, performance monitoring and evaluation aspects to strengthen fertilizer informatics for decision support. Information exchange for decision support has been promoted through Fertilizer Informatics Network (FERTNET) extended to Department of Fertilizers and various Fertilizer Companies viz. IFFCO, NFL, MFL, GNFC, FCI and HFCL.

6.10.13 Activities in the North-Eastern Region: Under the IT apparatus at the Field Offices and Directorates of DAC (DACNET), the following offices in the North-Eastern region have been covered:

1. Directorate of Marketing and Inspection at Guwahati and Shillong.
2. Central Integrated Pest Management Centres at Guwahati, Aizawl, Dimapur and Gangtok.
3. Regional Bio-fertilizer Development Centre at Imphal.
4. North-Eastern Regional Farm Machinery, Testing and Training Institute, Sonitpur, Assam.
5. Support under AGRISNET.

6.11 Computerisation of Agricultural Census and Input Survey

Recognizing the predominance of the agriculture sector in the Indian economy, Department of Agriculture and Cooperation collects and maintains agricultural statistics such as number, area, tenancy, land utilisation, cropping pattern and irrigation particulars of different classes of operational holdings regularly and make it timely accessible to the planners and policy makers for decision making. This project was entrusted to NIC and it made significant headway in almost all the States/UTs except Bihar, where Census is yet to be conducted. The salient features are the following:

1. Creation of large database of about 8,000 million bytes at National Level and 1 GB at state level.
2. Processing and tabulation of Agricultural Census and Input Survey database at District/State/National level.
3. Development and implementation of information retrieval system at micro and macro level for decision making at various levels.
4. Selective information will be put on Internet/Intranet for easy access of information to public to ensure transparency in the Government functioning.
5. Training programmes on software implementation for officers of States/UTs and Central Government.

To sum up, proper planning, monitoring and corrective action requires availability of timely information of right quality. The Central and State Governments require to hasten the process of computerisation of all the records and transactions. Since the government has a major say in promoting agriculture, this will have cascading effect on the entire rural areas. To begin with, it is necessary that the government agencies should accept conventional reports in the electronic format. This will bring about much desired speed and effectiveness in governance.

Many State Governments are showing interest in developing proper systems for e-governance. But the implementation of the same is still requires a lot to be desired. The Central and State Governments should also make information available for ready reference by those interested. This will be not only helpful to people but also will raise interest levels in IT-based services. Similarly, research institutions and NGOs should exchange and provide information through a well conceived network. These measures will encourage end user, i.e. farmer's participation and will provide the much needed input from them.

The Karnataka Government's Bhoomi project has led to the computerisation of the centuries-old system of handwritten rural land records. Through it, the revenue department has done away with the corruption-ridden system that involved bribing village accountants to procure land records; records of right, tenancy and cultivation certificates. The project is expected to benefit seventy lakh villagers in 30,000 villages.

A farmer can walk into the nearest taluk office and ask for a computer printout of his land record certificate for ₹ 15. He can also check details of land records on a touch-screen kiosk by inserting a two-rupee coin. These kiosks, installed at the taluk office, will provide the public with a convenient interface to the land records centre.

In this context, the Twelfth Five Year Plan (2012-17) remarked, "Already, a large number of services benefiting ordinary people have come into being. For a small fee, farmers can sign up for a service which provides customer specific information through SMS on market prices in nearby markets, conditions and possible disease outbreaks in specific crops in which the farmer is currently interested. Mobile banking, through business correspondents acting as agents, is giving ordinary people in villages, far from a brick and mortar bank branch, virtually direct access to simple banking service. There is scope for using the Universal Services Obligation Fund (USOF) creatively to enhance access to mobile telephone including especially as a platform for delivery of a range of services to the underserved in rural areas". [1]

Endnote

1. Government of India, Planning Commission, *Twelfth Five Year Plan* (2012-17), Volume I, Chapter 1, para 1.80.

7

Food and Nutritional Security

The pioneering work by agriculture scientists and the efforts of farmers had helped achieve a breakthrough in the agriculture sector in the 1960s, popularly known as the *Green Revolution*. High agricultural production and productivity achieved in subsequent years has been the main reason for attaining food security to a large extent. The country has not witnessed any big technological breakthrough in agriculture since then. The food safety net for each and every of the 121 crore (Census 2011) citizens—a number that is growing—requires enhanced agricultural production and productivity in the form of a Second Green Revolution.

Further, special attention is required for achieving higher production and productivity levels in pulses, oilseeds, fruits, and vegetables, which had remained untouched in the First Green Revolution but are essential for nutritional security. In this regard, achieving high production of poultry, meat and fisheries is also essential. The relatively weak supply responses to price hikes in agricultural commodities, especially food articles, in the recent past brings back into focus the central question of efficient supply chain management and need for sustained levels of growth in agriculture and allied sectors. The choice before the country is clear—to invest more in agriculture and allied sectors with the right strategies, policies, and interventions. This is also a necessary condition for inclusive growth and for ensuring that the benefits of growth reach a larger number of people.

7.1 Food Security Policy

Food security is one of the major components of social security. It consists of ensuring that food is available at all times, that all persons have means of and access to it, that it is nutritionally adequate in terms of quantity, quality and variety, and that it is acceptable within the given culture. There are three elements in this definition, availability, access and suitability. In recent years, nutrition has been considered as part of food security.

Public distribution system (PDS) is the cornerstone of Government's price policy and food security system in India. It ensures availability of certain essential commodities (sugar, kerosene, rice and wheat) at affordable prices, especially for the poor. Through its agency the Food Corporation of India (FCI), Government procures and stocks foodgrains, which are released every month for distribution through the PDS network across the country. These commodities are distributed to the public through a network of fair price shops (FPS). In addition to this, the system of procurement is also used by the Government to provide minimum support prices to the farmers in order to stabilise agricultural output and income.

India's food security policy was crafted with an aim to attain food self-sufficiency by making basic foodgrains available to all its citizens at affordable prices. To make this possible and to oversee its implementation, the Food Corporation of India (FCI) was set up under the Food Corporations Act, 1964. The FCI procures foodgrains from farmers at the Government declared minimum support price (MSP), stocks them in its warehouses, and then makes them available at affordable rates to the people through the public distribution system (PDS). PDS was restructured into the targeted public distribution system (TPDS) in 1997, under which issue price is different for those above and below the poverty line.

Besides the TPDS, the Government has implemented numerous other programmes aimed at food security, which include: (a) Integrated Child Development Scheme (ICDS) for providing nutrition and healthcare services to children and pregnant women, (b) Antyodaya Anna Yojana for providing affordable food to below poverty level (BPL) households, and

(c) Mid-day Meal Scheme for school children.

At the same time, the Government has been suppressing market prices through extensive restrictions and pricing controls on the free trade in foodgrains, and by providing input subsidies to farmers on water, power and fertilizers.

Over the years, India has successfully transformed itself from a foodgrains importing country to a food self-sufficient country with adequate buffer stocks to see itself through a year or two of bad agriculture.

Through a vast network of PDS outlets across the country, Government tries to deliver some minimal supplies of heavily subsidized foodgrains to below poverty line (BPL) households and also some above poverty line (APL) households. The PDS stores are first given subsidized foodgrains and then instructed to deliver them at below market price to specified households. At times, some unscrupulous storekeepers sell off subsidized foodgrains in the open market, and then adulterate the remaining foodgrains and sell the diluted product to BPL and APL households, who have no choice in the matter.

7.2 National Food Security Mission (NFSM), 2007

The National Development Council (NDC) in its 53rd meeting held on May 29, 2007 adopted a resolution to launch a Food Security Mission—comprising rice, wheat and pulses—to increase the production of rice by 10 million tons, wheat by 8 million tons and pulses by 2 million tons by the end of the Eleventh Five Year Plan (2011-12). Accordingly, a Centrally-sponsored scheme, viz. National Food Security Mission (NFSM) was launched from 2007-08 to operationalize the above mentioned resolution.

The approach is to bridge the yield gap in respect of these crops through dissemination of improved technologies and farm management practices. The scheme will focus on districts which have high potential but relatively low level of productivity at present. The mission aims at achieving its objectives through promotion and extension of improved technologies, i.e. seed, integrated nutrient management including micronutrients, soil amendments, integrated pest management and resource conservation technologies along with capacity building of farmers.

7.2.1 Components of NFSM: NFSM has the following 3 components:

1. National Food Security Mission—Rice (NFSM-Rice).
2. National Food Security Mission—Wheat (NFSM-Wheat).
3. National Food Security Mission—Pulses (NFSM-Pulses).

A series of activities for more vigorous promotion of pulse crops has been adopted under the NFSM to intensify the pulse production programme from 2010-11. These are as under:

1. Merging of the pulse component of the Integrated Scheme of Oilseeds, Pulses, Oil Palm and Maize (ISOPOM) with the NFSM so as to increase the scope and area coverage of the pulses programme. Jharkhand and Assam have also been included under the programme since there is immense potential for pulse promotion in rice fallows.
2. Through a new programme under the NFSM called the Accelerated Pulses Production Programme (A3P), 1000 block demonstrations of technology have been launched from 2010-11. This programme will essentially promote plant nutrients- and plant protection-centric technologies in compact blocks of 1,000 hectares each for 5 major pulse crops, namely tur, moong, urad, gram, and lentil.

7.2.2 Objectives of NFSM: These are the following:

1. Increasing production of rice, wheat and pulses through area expansion and productivity enhancement in a sustainable manner in the identified districts of the country.
2. Restoring soil fertility and productivity at the individual farm level.
3. Creating employment opportunities.
4. Enhancing farm level economy (i.e. farm profits) to restore confidence amongst the farmers.

7.2.3 Strategy to Achieve Objectives: To achieve the above objectives, NFSM would adopt the following strategies:

1. Implementation in a mission mode through active engagement of all the stakeholders at various levels.
2. Promotion and extension of improved technologies, i.e. seed, integrated nutrient management including micronutrients, soil amendments, integrated pest management and resource conservation technologies along with capacity building of farmers.
3. Flow of fund would be closely monitored to ensure that interventions reach the target beneficiaries on time.
4. Various interventions proposed would be integrated with the district plan and targets for each identified district would be fixed.
5. Constant monitoring and concurrent evaluation for assessing the impact of the interventions for a result oriented approach by the implementing agencies.

The scheme will be implemented through the Agricultural Technology Management Agency (ATMA) at the district level. The selection of beneficiaries and the identification of priority areas will be done by panchayati raj institutions (PRIs). At least 33 percent of the beneficiaries would be from small/marginal farmers. The allocation to SC/ST farmers would be in proportion to their population in the district. A beneficiary farmer would be entitled to avail assistance for area up to 2 hectares.

NFSM is currently running in 17 States of the country including Andhra Pradesh, Assam, Bihar, Chhattisgarh, Gujarat, Haryana, Jharkhand, Karnataka, Kerala, Madhya Pradesh, Maharashtra, Orissa, Punjab, Rajasthan, Tamil Nadu, Uttar Pradesh, and West Bengal.

7.2.4 Monitoring and Evaluation of NFSM: At the national level, 9 National Level Monitoring Teams (NLMTs) have been constituted with members drawn from various central and state organizations. All the 9 Crop Development Directorates of the Department of Agriculture and Co-operation, Ministry of Agriculture, Government of India are also monitoring the implementation of NFSM activities in the

17 NFSM States. Monitoring committees have also been constituted at state level and district level for monitoring the implementation of NFSM.

A Project Management Team has been appointed at national level for providing continuous technical supports to the states regarding formulation of action plans, implementation of various components prescribed under NFSM and also for monitoring the progress of various activities of NFSM through extensive field visits and technical guidance to the states.

Various monitoring/reporting formats (quarterly and annual) have been developed and issued to the states for obtaining the information about progress of NFSM activities. Handbooks on log frame analysis, reporting and monitoring formats, and criteria for selection of districts for awards have been prepared with the help of National Productivity Council for assisting the states in implementation and monitoring of the mission activities.

Management information system (MIS) for online submission of progress report at state, district and block level has been developed for maintaining transparency.

Farmers have enthusiastically responded to NFSM supported farm machinery components, especially to zero till seed drills, rotavators etc which is evident from the increased sale of these machines supported by NFSM. The awareness generated through demonstrations and distribution of seed minikits of newly released varieties to the farmers has triggered substantial increase in the use of high yielding varieties of wheat and rice seeds in identified districts. Capacity building exercises for farmers through Farmers Field Schools are also undertaken in orienting the farmers towards adoption of new agriculture technologies.

7.2.5 Revamped NFSM: NFSM is being implemented with the new target of additional production of 25 million tonnes of foodgrains comprising 10 million tonnes rice, 8 million tonnes wheat, 4 million tonnes pulses, and 3 million tonnes coarse cereals by the end of the Twelfth Five Year Plan (2016-17). The revamped NFSM is being implemented from 2014-15 in 619 districts of 28 states. In addition to rice, wheat and pulses, crops like coarse cereals and commercial crops (sugarcane, cotton, and jute) have been included since 2014-15. Promotion of farmer producer organizations (FPOs), value addition, dal mill, and assistance for custom hiring charges have also been undertaken under the Mission. The pulses component has been allocated 50 percent of total funds under the NFSM in order to increase their production. To promote the use of bio-fertilizers, subsidy on bio-fertilizer has also been enhanced from ₹ 100 per hectare to ₹ 300 per hectare.

7.3 National Food Security Act, 2013

In his budget speech to the Parliament on February 28, 2011, the Finance Minister Pranab Mukerjee stated, "After detailed consultations with all stakeholders including State Governments, we are close to the finalisation of National Food Security Bill (NFSB) which will be introduced in the Parliament during the course of this year".

National Food Security Bill was introduced in the Lok Sabha on December 22, 2011. After its introduction in the Lok Sabha, the Bill was referred to the Parliamentary Standing Committee on Food, Consumer Affairs and Public Distribution for examination. The Committee held wide ranging consultations with Central Ministries/Departments, various other organizations and individuals and also visited States/UTs to obtain their views/suggestions on the Bill. The Standing Committee submitted its report to the Speaker, Lok Sabha on January 17, 2013, which was processed in consultation with concerned Central Ministries/Departments and States/UTs. This highly controversial legislation was passed only in late August 2013, after initially being promulgated as a presidential ordinance on July 5, 2013.

7.3.1 Background: India's high economic growth rate in recent years has not been fully reflected in the health status of its people, with 22 percent of its population undernourished.

According to the National Family Health Survey 2005-06, 40.4 percent of children under the age of three are underweight, 33 percent of women in the age group of 15-49 have a body mass index below normal and 78.9 percent of children in the age group of 6-35 months are anaemic. These are disturbing statistics which point to nutritional deficiencies. National Food Security Act, 2013 is designed to address these deficiencies in India.

It is at times assumed that the relationship between economic growth and health is uni-directional in the sense that improvement in economic conditions leads to better health. In reality, the reverse is equally true, i.e. health is an *economic engine*. In other words, better health—which is an important end in itself—leads to and may, in certain cases, be a necessary pre-requisite for economic development. Hence, the economic role of health and nutrition provides an additional and compelling rationale for public policy to support well-targeted nutrition improving interventions.

Indian National Food Security Act, 2013 (also Right to Food Act), was signed into law on September 12, 2013. This law aims to provide subsidized foodgrains to 67 percent (approximately two-thirds) of India's 121 crore people.

Food security means availability of sufficient foodgrains to meet the domestic demand as well as access, at the individual level, to adequate quantities of food at affordable prices. The Act marks a paradigm shift in addressing the problem of food security—from the current welfare approach to a right-based approach. About two-thirds of the population will be entitled to receive subsidized foodgrains under Targeted Public Distribution System—India's principal domestic food aid programme

The Act has been termed as biggest ever experiment in the world for distributing highly subsidized food by any government through a rights-based approach.

Under the provisions of the Act, beneficiaries are entitled to purchase 5 kilograms per eligible person per month of cereals at the following prices: Rice at ₹ 3 per kilogram, wheat at ₹ 2 per kilogram and coarse grains (millet) at ₹ 1 per kilogram. Pregnant women, lactating mothers, and certain categories of children are eligible for daily free meals. The Act provides for penalty for non-compliance by public servants.

7.3.2 Salient Features of the Act: These are as under:

1. 75 percent of rural and 50 percent of the urban population are entitled for 3 years (from enactment) to 5 kilograms of foodgrains per month at ₹ 3, ₹ 2, ₹ 1 per kilogram for rice, wheat and coarse grains (millet), respectively.
2. The work of identification of eligible households has been left to the State Governments.
3. Pregnant women and lactating mothers are entitled to a nutritious *take home ration* of 600 calories and a maternity benefit of at least ₹ 6,000 for 6 months.
4. Children 6 months to 14 years of age are to receive free hot meals or *take home rations.*
5. Central Government will provide funds to State Governments in case of short supplies of foodgrains.
6. Current foodgrains allocation of the States will be protected by the Central Government for at least 6 months.
7. State Governments will provide a food security allowance to the beneficiaries in case of non-supply of foodgrains.
8. Public Distribution System (PDS) is to be reformed.
9. Eldest woman in the household, 18 years or above, will be the head of the household for the issuance of the ration card.
10. There will be state- and district-level redress mechanisms.
11. State Food Commissions will be formed for implementation and monitoring of the provisions of the Act.

7.3.3 Main Provisions of the Act: These are as under:

A. Preliminaries: The Act extends to the whole of India and "shall be deemed to have come into force on the 5th day of July 2013" (this is the date when the National Food Security Ordinance 2013 came into force).

B. Entitlements:

(a) Public Distribution System (PDS): Priority households are entitled to 5 kilograms of foodgrains per person per month, and Antyodaya households to 35 kilograms per household per month. The combined coverage of Priority and Antyodaya households (called *eligible households*) shall extend *up to 75 percent of the rural population and up to 50 percent of the urban population*. The PDS issue prices are given in Schedule I: ₹ 3/2/1 per kilogram for rice/wheat/millets. These may be revised after 3 years.

(b) Children's Entitlements: Entitlements for children are as shown in Table 7.1.

Table 7.1: Children's Entitlements

For children in the age group of 6 months to 6 years.	An age-appropriate meal, free of charge, through the local anganwadi.
For children aged 6-14 years.	One free mid-day meal every day (except on school holidays) in all government and government-aided schools, up to Class VIII.
For children below six months.	Exclusive breastfeeding shall be promoted.
For children who suffer from malnutrition.	Meals will be provided to them free of charge through the local anganwadi.

(c) Entitlements of Pregnant and Lactating Women: Every pregnant and lactating mother is entitled to a free meal at the local *anganwadi* (during pregnancy and 6 months after child birth) as well as maternity benefits of ₹ 6,000, in instalments.

The entitlements of women and children are to be delivered by State Governments through schemes in accordance with guidelines to be prescribed by the Central Government.

C. Identification of Eligible Households: The Act does not specify criteria for the identification of households eligible for PDS entitlements. The Central Government is to determine the state-wise coverage of the PDS (proportion of the rural/urban population). Then number of eligible persons will be calculated from Census population figures. The identification of eligible households is left to State Governments, subject to the scheme's guidelines for Antyodaya, and subject to guidelines to be specified by the State Government for Priority households. The identification of eligible households is to be completed within 365 days. The lists of eligible households are to be placed in the public domain and "displayed prominently".

D. State Food Commissions: The Act provides for the creation of State Food Commissions. The main function of a State Food Commission will be: (a) to monitor the implementation of the Act, (b) give advice to the State Government and its agencies and (c) inquire into violations of entitlements.

State Food Commissions will also hear appeals against orders of the District Grievance Redressal Officer and prepare annual reports.

E. Transparency and Grievance Redressal: The Act provides for a two-tier grievance redressal structure, involving the District Grievance Redressal Officer (DGRO) and State Food Commission. State Governments must also put in place an internal grievance redressal mechanism which may include call centres, helplines etc.

(a) Transparency Provisions: Mandatory transparency provisions include the following:

1. Placing all PDS-related records in the public domain.
2. Conducting periodic social audits of the PDS and other welfare schemes.
3. Using information and communication technology to ensure transparent recording of transactions at all levels.
4. Setting up vigilance committees at all levels to supervise all schemes under the Act.

(b) District Grievance Redressal Officers (DGROs): DGROs shall be appointed by State Governments for each district to hear complaints and take necessary action according to norms to be prescribed by State Governments. If a complainant is not satisfied, he or she may file an appeal before the State Food Commission.

(c) Penalties and Compensation: A State Food Commission has powers to impose penalties. If an order of the DGRO is not complied with, the concerned authority or officer can be fined up to ₹ 5,000. The Commission can authorise any of its members to act as an adjudicating officer for this purpose. In case of non-supply of the entitled quantities of foodgrains or meals to entitled persons, such persons will be entitled to a food security allowance from the State Government, as prescribed by the Central Government.

F. Other Provisions: These are as under:

(a) PDS Reforms: In Chapter V, the Act states that Central and State Governments "shall endeavour to progressively undertake" various PDS reforms, including the following:

1. Doorstep delivery of foodgrains.
2. End-to-end computerization.
3. Leveraging "aadhaar" (UID) for unique identification of entitled beneficiaries.
4. Full transparency of records.
5. Preference to public institutions or bodies in licensing of fair price shops.
6. Management of fair price shops by women or their collectives.
7. Diversification of commodities distributed under the PDS.
8. Introduction of schemes such as cash transfer, food coupons or other schemes to the targeted beneficiaries in order to ensure their foodgrains entitlements as prescribed by the Central Government.

(b) Obligations of Government and Local Authorities: The main obligation of the Central Government is to provide foodgrains (or, failing that, funds) to State Governments, at prices specified in Schedule I, to implement the main entitlements. The Central Government has wide-ranging powers to make Rules in consultation with the State Governments.

The main obligation of State Governments is to implement the relevant schemes, in accordance with the Central Government guidelines. State Governments also have wide-ranging powers to make Rules. They are free to extend benefits and entitlements beyond what is prescribed in the Act, from their own resources.

Local authorities and panchayati raj institutions are responsible for proper implementation of the Act in their respective areas, and may be given additional responsibilities by notification.

G. Schedules: The Act has the following four schedules (which can be amended by notification).

1. Schedule I prescribes issue prices for the PDS.
2. Schedule II prescribes nutritional standards for mid-day meals, take-home rations and related entitlements.
3. Schedule III lists various provisions for advancing food security.
4. Schedule IV specifies a minimum foodgrains allocation for each state, in the case of states that might lose otherwise under the Act. This essentially means continuing of existing allocations.

7.3.4 Critical Assessment: For proponents, food security is a form of investment in human capital. It will bring some security in people's lives and make it easier for them to meet their basic needs, protect their health, educate their children, and take risks.

Criticism of the Act includes accusations of both political motivation and fiscal irresponsibility. According to some, food prices are still elevated and the food security Act will aggravate food price inflation as it will tilt supply towards cereals and away from other farm produce (proteins), which will raise food prices further. It is also feared that the legislation would: (a) restrict private initiative in agriculture, (b) reduce competition in the marketplace due to government domination of the grain market, (c) shift money from investments in agriculture to subsidies and (d) continue focus on cereals production when shifts in consumer demand patterns indicate a need to focus more on protein, fruits and vegetables.

7.4 Forests and Food Security

Food security is the outcome of complex interactions among natural resource management, political, social, and economic factors. Forests, as an important element within this matrix, affect food security in three major areas.

7.4.1 Forests and Agriculture: Forests help maintain favourable and stable conditions needed for sustained agricultural productivity. Moisture and nutrient leaching from the adjoining forests maintain the fertility of the agriculture fields. It is common in forest regions of Eastern India plateau (Northern Odisha, Jharkhand, and Eastern Chhattisgarh) for farmers to desist from the use of chemical fertilizers. Thus, many farmers leave their fields near a moderately dense forest to be fed entirely from moisture and nutrient from the forests and save the precious cow dung to fertilize more distant fields.

Over the years, local communities have developed sophisticated indigenous techniques to augment and harvest forest-based moisture and nutrient flow. Raised bunds on forest boundaries along the contours are common in the Eastern India plateau. Further, in recent years a cash rich economy has developed in many forest areas when farmers found out that fields at the foot of the forested hills are best suited for potato cultivation, as these have accumulated rich potash deposit that has leached down from the uphill forests.

Windbreaks and shelterbelts protect crops from drying and damaging winds. Local people fully appreciate the importance of forests in disease control and prevention of epidemic outbreak related to agriculture crops. Local villagers in forested regions appreciate the role of avifauna in the control of rodent and insect pests. Forests also serve as the chief source of tree fodder for feeding livestock. Of growing importance is the role forests play as storehouses of biodiversity, potentially very important in future crop breeding and pest and disease management programmes.

7.4.2 Forest Foods: Forest foods are important for the local villagers during both stress and normal periods, and the use of forest foods as a component of local response strategies to increasing food insecurity is widely documented. In normal times, leafy vegetables, mushroom, berries and fruits available in different seasons form the usual component of their diet. Having a diverse resource base with a range of different trees, plants and insect species, forests increase the options for maintaining food security. Different seasonal products complement each other with seasonally different pattern of availability. Leafy vegetables and fruits provide essential vitamins and minerals as dietary supplements. Similarly, wild fruits are very rich in Vitamin A and C.

Moreover, the forest foods have a definite pro-poor bias. Women and children are the largest consumers, followed by the elderly. In the wake of social customs forcing rural women to eat at the end—and at times only the left over and poor portions of the cooked meal—such harvests do help women regain some nutrition. During the periods of acute food shortage, forest foods sustain livelihoods.

7.4.3 Forests and Fisheries: Forests also have significant links with inland and marine fisheries. Rivers and streams are rich fishing grounds for local populations. Forests regulate the volume and fluctuations of stream flows and provide a shaded riparian environment favourable for the development of smaller life forms which fish feed on. Villagers in the forest region of Eastern India plateau know that the water flowing from bamboo forests has high nutrient capacity and is able to support larger volumes and healthy population of edible aquatic fauna (fish, crab, mussel, snail etc.).

The mangrove swamps in southern India provide habitats for many fish species, especially shrimps. The fish catch from these areas not only enriches protein-deficient diets and generates household income, but also helps maintain/enrich local level social capital when the whole village gathers to celebrate community fish harvesting festivals based on the principles of strict equality in sharing of the catch.

7.5 Food Safety and Standards Authority of India (FSSAI)

The Food Safety and Standards Act passed by Parliament in 2006 provides for consolidation and replacement of the following erstwhile laws relating to food:

1. Prevention of Food Adulteration Act, 1954.
2. Fruit Products Order, 1955.
3. Meat Food Products Order, 1973.
4. Vegetable Oil Products (Control) Order, 1947.
5. Edible Oils Packaging (Regulation) Order, 1998.
6. Milk and Milk Products Order, 1992.
7. Other orders issued under the Essential Commodities Act, 1955 relating to food.

All food business operators (FBOs) other than petty food businesses are required to obtain a Central or a State license depending upon the provisions of the Act. The petty FBOs have to obtain registration. The Act and the regulations thereunder are enforced by the Central Food Authority, viz. FSSAI and at the State level by Food Safety Commissioners for each State, Designated Officers for each District and Food Safety Officers for local areas as assigned by the respective Food Safety Commissioner. The enforcement agencies enjoy powers to issue or cancel license of food business operators, prohibit the sale of any article of food which is not as per prescribed standards, to inspect units and to take samples, to seize any articles of food which appear to be in contravention of the Act or the regulations, to levy penalty and to launch prosecution.

While the FSS Act empowers FSSAI and the State level authorities, the infrastructure to administer the Act is still not in place. There is a general lack of awareness about the Act and the regulations, especially among the small businesses. A number of small FBOs have expressed concern over the regulatory compliance of registration and approval for proprietary products for opening and running business. There is a need to have a broad-based consultation with all stakeholders for implementation of the various provisions of law to ensure that the growth of food business does not retard.

FSSAI was established under Food Safety and Standards (FSS) Act, 2006 which consolidated various Acts and orders that had hitherto handled food-related issues in various Ministries/Departments of the Government of India. FSSAI was created for laying down science-based standards for articles of food and to regulate their manufacture, storage, distribution, sale and import, to ensure availability of safe and wholesome food for human consumption.

The Act also aims to establish a single reference point for all matters relating to food safety and standards, by moving from multi-level, multi-departmental control to a single line of command. To this effect, the Act established an independent statutory authority, viz. Food Safety and Standards Authority of India (FSSAI) with head office in Delhi. FSSAI and the State Food Safety Authorities enforce various provisions of the Act.

Ministry of Health and Family Welfare, Government of India is the Administrative Ministry for FSSAI.

FSSAI has been mandated by the FSS Act, 2006 to perform the following functions:

1. Framing of Regulations to lay down the Standards and guidelines in relation to articles of food and specifying appropriate system of enforcing various standards thus notified.
2. Laying down mechanisms and guidelines for accreditation of certification bodies engaged in certification of food safety management system for food businesses.
3. Laying down procedure and guidelines for accreditation of laboratories and notification of the accredited laboratories.

4. Providing scientific advice and technical support to Central Government and State Governments in the matters of framing the policy and rules in areas which have a direct or indirect bearing of food safety and nutrition.
5. Collecting and collating data regarding food consumption, incidence and prevalence of biological risk, contaminants in food, residues of various, contaminants in foods products, identification of emerging risks and introduction of rapid alert system.
6. Creating an information network across the country so that the public, consumers, Panchayats etc receive rapid, reliable and objective information about food safety and issues of concern.
7. Providing training programmes for persons who are involved or intend to get involved in food businesses.
8. Contributing to the development of international technical standards for food, sanitary and phyto-sanitary standards.
9. Promoting general awareness about food safety and food standards.

7.6 SAARC Food Security Reserve (Food Bank)

The agreement on establishing the SAARC (South Asian Association for Regional Cooperation) Food Bank came into force on August 12, 1988. The Food Bank would act as a regional food security reserve for the SAARC member countries during normal time food shortages and emergencies. The Agreement contains broad principles for determination of price. The prices, terms and conditions of payment in respect of foodgrains would be the subject of direct negotiation between the concerned member countries based on the guidelines for price determination to be approved by the Food Bank Board periodically. The Agreement sought to rationalize and improve the provisions on the procedures for withdrawal and release of foodgrains. It delineates the role of the Board to administer functioning of the Food Bank and its policymaking, distinct from the designated nodal point(s) responsible for transacting the entire business at the national level related to operations of the Food Bank.

In view of the emerging global situation of reduced food availability and a worldwide rise in food prices, a meeting of the Agriculture Ministers of the SAARC member states was held in New Delhi, India in November 2008, to evolve and implement people-centred short to medium term regional strategy and collaborative projects that would, among others, lead to the following:

1. Increase in food production.
2. Investment in agriculture and agro-based industries.
3. Agriculture research and prevention of soil health degradation.
4. Development and sharing of agricultural technologies.
5. Sharing of best practices in procurement and distribution.
6. Management of the climatic and disease-related risks in agriculture.

To sum up, at the time of Independence the country faced two major nutritional problems; one was the threat of famine and acute starvation due to low agricultural production and lack of appropriate food distribution system. The other was chronic energy deficiency due to poverty, low-literacy, poor access to safe-drinking water, sanitation and health care; these factors led to wide spread prevalence of infections and ill health in children and adults.

During the last 70 years, considerable progress has been achieved. Famines no longer stalk the country. There has been substantial reduction in moderate and severe under-nutrition in children and some improvement in nutritional status of all segments of population. In view of the fact that population growth in India will continue for the next few decades, it is essential that appropriate strategies are devised to improve food and nutrition security of families.

The food and nutritional security of India currently depends to a great extent on the production of wheat and rice. These two crops together constituted 78 percent of total foodgrains production in 2009-10, whereas coarse cereals constitute only 15 percent in the same year. The nutritional value of coarse cereals is also gradually being realized. There is every reason to promote the production of these crops and help them realize their full potential with increased investment in research and schemes to promote their cultivation particularly in rain-fed areas.

Presently, there are marketable surpluses of foodgrains in India. The prevalence of widespread hunger is not due to the non-availability of food in the market but due to lack of adequate purchasing power among the rural and urban poor. Inadequate purchasing power, in turn, is due to insufficient opportunities for gainful employment. The famines of jobs and of purchasing power are becoming the primary causes for the famines of food in the households of the poor. Poverty, increased food consumption, land degradation, climate change are some of the causes of food insecurity.

Food security of India is closely related to development of technologies for increasing the agriculture outputs through process innovations for land saving and water use. The question is how to develop and deploy new agro biotechnology tools and precision agriculture for increasing the output of agriculture sector in the country.

8

Gender Issues in Indian Agriculture

Improving the status and treatment of women is a major development challenge. On January 22, 2015, the Prime Minister launched the *Beti Bachao, Beti Padhao* campaign from Panipat in Haryana. The campaign is aimed at increasing the low value that Indian society puts on a girl child.

Gender discrimination in India, embedded in the social fabric, has various dimensions:

1. It starts from the womb with sex determination tests and abortion of the female fetuses.
2. Discrimination in terms of nutrition offered to the girl child.
3. Length and type of schooling the girl child avails of vis-à-vis her male siblings.
4. Inadequate or lack of access to higher education.
5. Discrimination in opportunities of employment and wages paid.
6. Unequal share in inheritance.

Government has relied on the legal route to address each of these discriminations, without matching changes in the social fabric or role model set by leaders in society from all spheres. The legal route suffers from several shortcomings, especially in terms of time taken for dispensation of justice. For each of the above discrimination, there is a law so all acts of discrimination are illegal. However, compliance requires a lot more to be done.

8.1 Role of Women in Agriculture

Rural women form the most important productive work force in the Indian economy. Beyond the conventional market-oriented narrower definition of *productive workers*, almost all women in rural India can be considered as *farmers* in some sense, working as agricultural labourers, unpaid workers in the family farm enterprise, or combination of the two. Moreover, several farm activities traditionally carried out by men are also being undertaken by women as men are pulled away into higher paying employment. Thus, rural India is witnessing a process which could be described as feminization of agriculture.

Despite significant contribution of women in the production process, an all pervasive bias of development planners in treating them primarily as consumers of social services rather than producers, kept them away from the development programmes in agriculture and allied sectors. As men and women have different roles and needs and face gender-specific constraints, women may not automatically benefit from development activities, but may remain excluded.

Similarly, in spite of key role of women in crop husbandry, animal husbandry, fisheries, forestry and post-harvest technology, those in-charge of formulating packages of technologies, services and public policies for rural areas have often tended to neglect the productive role of women. Consequently, the developments of technologies, specifically tailored to women-specific occupations and the involvement of women in technology development and transfer have received inadequate attention from both scientific and administrative departments of Government.

Women have traditionally been discriminated in their access to productive resources and have been denied ownership of land, cattle, trees, harvest and shelter. They have even been discriminated in access to credit and marketing facilities for their economic activities. It is, thus, essential to develop strategies and mechanism to improve women's access to agricultural support services.

It has been recognized that for an accelerated socio-economic development of any community, the active participation of women in the entire process is very essential. In a social set up like ours, the participation of women in the development process has to be ensured through tangible measures, taken at various levels, which result in empowerment of women in the real sense. In view of the above, government has taken a conscious view to make adequate provisions in its policies and programmes through which it is to be ensured that the women of the country are empowered and they become the active participants in the development process.

The absence of faster diversification is partly due to the lack of new economic opportunities for women. While men migrate as well as take up new employment opportunities in rural areas, women find themselves at a disadvantage.

There appears to be a faster rate of occupational mobility out of agriculture among men than among women. The latter remain more bound to rural areas and to agriculture due to socio-cultural and structural causes.

8.2 Importance of Land for Women

Land is important for women due to following reasons:

1. Land access can reduce a household's risk of poverty, but for persistent gender inequalities land solely in men's hands need not guarantee female welfare.
2. Direct land transfers to women are likely to benefit not just women but also children. Evidence, both from India and from many other parts of the world, shows that women, especially in poor households, spend most of the earnings they control on basic household needs, while men spend a significant part of theirs on personal goods, such as alcohol, tobacco etc.
3. Women with assets such as land have greater bargaining power, which can lead to more gender-equal allocations of benefits even from male incomes.
4. Women without independent resources are highly vulnerable to poverty and destitution in case of desertion, divorce, or widowhood. In parts of western and north-western India, rural women even from rich parental and marital families, deprived of their property shares when

widowed, can be found working as agricultural labourers on the farms of their well-off brothers or brothers-in-law. The fate of deserted and divorced women is worse.

5. Tenure security, and especially titles, can empower women to assert themselves better with agencies that provide inputs and extension services.
6. Women in many parts of South Asia are often better informed than men about traditional seed varieties and the attributes of trees and grasses. If they have greater control over land and farming, this knowledge can be put to better use.

8.2.1 Sources of Land for Women: There are three main sources of land for women:

1. Direct government transfers.
2. Market purchase/lease.
3. Inheritance or gifts from families.

To enhance women's land access from all three sources, a range of initiatives are needed, including land titles to women in all government land transfers, credit support to poor women to purchase or lease in land from the market, raising legal awareness and legal support about women's inheritance rights.

It will also need a new approach to enable women to retain the land they get by strongly encouraging a *group approach* in land cultivation and investment in productive assets. It is now well-recognized that the poor are best empowered if they function as a group rather than as individuals. This lesson should be incorporated in the creation of all productive assets in women's hands.

Agricultural policies are of prime importance in gender budgeting exercises as there is a growing feminization of agriculture in recent years with out-migration of men to urban areas in search of work. The number of women-headed households in the agricultural sector is also increasing. The prosperity of agriculture therefore will largely depend on how effectively these women are empowered.

Enhancing women's rights to land, providing infrastructure

support to women farmers and advancing legal support on existing laws are some of the policy interventions needed. However, critical problems persist. The lack of formal titles to women on the land they cultivate is a big drawback. This adversely affects their access to credit, inputs and marketing outlets. It also reinforces women's position as unpaid farm labourers, which reduces their incentives to invest in the land. It further excludes them from receiving agricultural extension services, new production techniques etc.

The lack of appropriate women-friendly tools and agricultural implements is another drawback. Also, the co-operatives of farmers basically comprise of men and therefore disadvantageous to women in terms of mindset and location and services profile. The agricultural policy, therefore, needs to be reviewed to provide a gender-friendly perspective.

Policies for non-farm sector and information are another highly important area that has to be seriously reviewed keeping in view the gender perspective. As women tend to remain in the rural sector they also undertake non-farm activities, which significantly contribute to the family's income. In times of agricultural stress, it is these non-farm activities of women that support the family. Therefore, the requirements of women in this sector need to be identified and appropriate support facilities in terms of access to raw materials, micro credit, skill development, training, market linkages etc. have to be ensured.

8.2.2 Hindu Succession (Amendment) Act, 2005: It made significant amendments in the Hindu Succession Act, 1956 correcting existing inequities in women's rights to agricultural land, Mitakshara joint family property, parental dwelling house and certain widow rights. This has brought woman on par with men in relation to agricultural land.

8.3 Gender-sensitive Agricultural Policies of the Government

8.3.1 Resettlement and Rehabilitation Policy: The process of involuntary resettlement as a result of large development projects often leads to loss of land, wage employment, and housing and shelter, calling for gender-sensitive plans toward land-based re-settlement, re-employment and re-construction of houses. For instance, women should also get legal rights to land allocated as part of a resettlement package. Women's livelihood and economic activities—be they gathering forest produce, working in the fields or selling agricultural, animal husbandry, forestry or fishery produce—need to be enumerated so that the resettlement and rehabilitation plan also makes provision for the restoration of their livelihood and income. Women's views need to be solicited regarding houses, toilets, water and sanitation.

The process of displacement and involuntary resettlement also leads to increased stress, psychological trauma, increasing exposure to parasitic and vector-borne diseases and to social evils and violence. Endemic infections may lead to the death of children and the elderly in the care of women. Alcoholism, gambling and prostitution and increase in the incidence of sexual abuse and violence as a result of large-scale dislocation of peoples adversely affect women in ways different from that of men. Involuntary resettlement also increases the risk that the affected household may fall into chronic food insecurity. Loss of common property resources (CPRs) like access to forests, water bodies and grazing lands are often disregarded by planners and are not compensated for. Loss of CPRs leads to women spending more time and energy accessing fuel, fodder and potable water. Involuntary resettlement also leads to loss of social status as a result of loss of community networks and social marginalisation. Women are affected, more deeply and differently than men, because they generally have lower levels of skills and education and have a limited social exposure. Women rely on community networks for emotional and practical support, for example, taking care of the children, and thus the dislocation of community networks can be traumatic for them. Community services and assets need to be restored and social networks and communities need to be rebuilt in consultation and with the active participation of women.

The fact that the impact of dislocation is different for

women needs to be understood and mitigated. Also, in drawing up resettlement and rehabilitation plans, care should be taken to see that widows, elderly persons, divorced women and women-headed households do not suffer a loss of their rights as a result of patriarchal biases. Detailed studies of the impact of development projects, say large dams, on women's lives, especially regarding resettlement and rehabilitation need to be sponsored, which can then be used to formulate a gender-sensitive resettlement and rehabilitation policy. The issue of a gender-sensitive resettlement and rehabilitation policy has not been addressed and this deserves immediate public attention.

In short, the absence of faster diversification is partly due to the lack of new economic opportunities for women. While men migrate as well as take up new employment opportunities in rural areas, women find themselves at a disadvantage. There appears to be a faster rate of occupational mobility out of agriculture among men than among women. The latter remain more bound to rural areas and to agriculture due to socio-cultural and structural causes. The faster shift out of agriculture among male workers compared to female workers is expected to result in what is termed as feminization of the agricultural workforce.

8.3.2 National Gender Resource Centre in Agriculture (NGRCA): In line with the National Agriculture Policy, 2000, policy level initiatives for gender mainstreaming are being promoted by the Ministry Agriculture, Government of India. NGRCA was set up during 2004-05 under the Scheme of Extension Support to Central Institutes to reflect the national commitment of empowerment of women through the 'strategy of mainstreaming and agenda setting'. The Centre acts as a focal point for the convergence of gender-related activities and issues in agriculture and allied sectors, for adding gender dimension to agriculture policies and programmes, and for rendering advocacy/advisory services to the States/UTs to internalize gender-specific interventions for bringing the farm women in the mainstream of agriculture development.

Similarly, to bring gender concerns on to the centre stage in all aspects of public expenditure and policy, a Gender Budgeting Cell has been constituted in the Ministry of Agriculture to look into the budgetary commitments of its various schemes and ensure a proportionate flow of the public expenditure to benefit women farmers. It has been mandated that a minimum of 30 percent funds would be utilized for women farmers under all the beneficiary-oriented programmes and schemes. Division-wise identified nodal officers/gender co-ordinators have been sensitized about the concept of gender budgeting.

Besides promoting mainstreaming of gender issues, the NGRCA has also taken other initiatives, which include the following:

1. Undertaking macro/micro level action research studies in critical thrusts areas including assessment of gender content and the impact of various on-going programmes and schemes and to make appropriate recommendations, if required, on strategy and design of schemes to incorporate gender perspective.
2. Collecting, analyzing and documenting success stories of women farmers.
3. Assessing gender content and generating *gender disaggregated data* in respect of various schemes and programmes.
4. To utilize gender sensitization modules (GSM) for sensitizing extension functionaries at different levels, namely senior, middle and cutting-edge level.
5. To revise reporting and monitoring formats to generate gender disaggregated data.

As a part of its networking strategies, NGRCA is committed to initiate appropriate actions related to agriculture on the recommendations of National Policy for Empowerment of Women (NPEW) formulated by the Ministry of Women and Child Development (MW&CD) and other agencies working for gender equality and fighting against social evils.

8.3.3 National Policy for Farmers (NPF), 2007: NPF announced by the Government envisages the following measures aimed at women's empowerment.

1. Asset reforms under land, water, and livestock for an equitable share to women farmers.
2. Better access to inputs and services science and technology, implements, credit and support services like crèches, child care centres, nutrition, health and training.
3. Encouragement to women for participating in group activities aimed at achieving economies of scale through farming groups.
4. Involvement of women in conservation and development of bio-resources.

8.3.4 Mahila Kissan Shasaktikaran Pariyojana (MKSP): In order to improve the present status of women in agriculture, and to enhance the opportunities for their empowerment, Government of India has announced MKSP as a sub-component of National Rural Livelihoods Mission (NRLM). MKSP recognizes the centrality of women in agriculture and therefore aims to provide direct and indirect support to enable them to achieve sustainable agriculture production. It will initiate a learning cycle by which women are enabled to learn and adopt appropriate technologies and farming systems. MKSP will be implemented as a sub-component of NRLM through specially formulated projects.

The salient features of MKSP are as follows:

1. Primary objective of MKSP is to empower women in agriculture by making systematic investments to enhance their participation and productivity in agriculture-based livelihood.
2. Through this scheme, it is proposed to create sustainable agricultural livelihood opportunities for women in agriculture and in the process ensure food and nutrition security at the household and the community levels.
3. Under MKSP, community-based women institutions in the rural area will be strengthened in order to enable them to

manage their agriculture-based livelihood activities.

4. Under MKSP, use of locally-adopted resource conserving, farmer-led and environmentally-friendly technologies has been emphasized.
5. Ministry of Rural Development, Government of India would provide funding support or up to 75 percent (90 percent for North East and hill states) to the project submitted by the State Government/Project Implementing Agencies (PIAs) under MKSP. Balance is to be contributed by the respective State Governments or any other donor agencies.

The expected outcomes of MKSP are as follows:

1. Net increase in the income of women in agriculture on a sustainable basis.
2. Improvement in food and nutritional security of women in agriculture and their families.
3. Increase in area under cultivation, cropping intensity and food production by women.
4. Increased levels of skill and performance by women in agriculture.
5. Increased access of women in agriculture to productive land, inputs, credit, technology and information.
6. Drudgery reduction for women in agriculture through use or gender friendly tools/technologies.
7. Increased access to market and market information for better marketing of their product.
8. Increased soil health and fertility to sustain agriculture based livelihoods.
9. Increased visibility of women in agriculture as an interest group.

9

Climate Change and Indian Agriculture

Climate change impacts on agriculture are being witnessed all over the world, but countries like India are more vulnerable in view of higher demographic pressure on natural resources and poor coping up mechanisms. Models generally predict that rising temperatures, increased climate variability and extreme weather events could significantly affect food production in the coming decades. Climate change is a serious global environmental concern, which is primarily caused by the building up of greenhouse gases in the atmosphere. Recent discourse on climate change has underscored the fact that climate change occupies a high priority on the environmental agenda of international community.

Global climate change due to rising levels of green house gases (GHGs) in the atmosphere is one of the most serious environmental concerns of present time. The accumulated scientific evidence clearly indicates that if the rate of GHG emissions is not reduced very significantly, there will be a damaging effect on the global climate.

Since global warming is caused by total accumulation of GHG and each country's emissions add to the stock, the cost of each country's emissions is borne by the entire global community. Similarly, the benefits of reduction in emission by any one country accrue not to the country itself but to the entire global community. This is classically a situation characterized by externalities in which individual countries will not have a sufficient incentive to undertake mitigation unless all countries co-operate in what is felt to be a collective effort with an equitable distribution of the burden of reducing emissions.

9.1 Evidence on Climate Change

The Intergovernmental Panel on Climate Change (IPCC), established in 1988 by the World Meteorological Organization (WMO) and the United Nations Environment Programme (UNEP), has worked extensively on evaluating past trends and the future prospects of climate change. IPCC reviews and assesses the most recent scientific, technical, and socio-economic information produced worldwide relevant to climate change.

According to IPCC, the global temperature may rise by 2-4.5 degree centigrade by the end of this century, including a 2.7-4.3°C increase over India by 2080s if adequate actions are not taken to reduce emissions globally. At the national level, the observed increase in surface air temperatures over the past century is 0.4 degree centigrade.

9.1.1 The Fourth Assessment Report (AR4) of IPCC, 2007: AR4 of IPCC, released in November 2007, concluded that the fact of global warming is unequivocal and there is enough evidence to indicate that this is due to anthropogenic reasons. Recent years have been the warmest since 1860, the year from when regular instrumental records are available. It is important to note that global warming will affect mankind seriously.

AR4 of IPCC brought climate change issue to the fore and led the parties to make serious efforts to address the problem through long-term cooperative actions as agreed under the Bali Action Plan. IPCC made serious projections of the future scenario in terms of global warming and predicted that there may be adverse impact of climate change on agriculture, water resources, eco-systems, sea levels, human health and result in rise in extreme weather events.

9.1.2 Fifth Assessment Report (AR5) of IPCC, 2014: IPCC in its AR5 observed that there has been an increasing trend in the anthropogenic emissions of greenhouse gases (GHGs) since the advent of the industrial revolution, with about half of the anthropogenic CO_2 emissions during this period occurring in the last 40 years. The period 1983-2012 is likely to have been the warmest 30 year period of the last

1,400 years. CO_2 emissions from fossil fuel combustion and industrial processes have contributed a major portion of total GHG emissions during the period 1970-2010.

The change in the climate system is likely to have adverse impact on the economy, livelihoods, cropping pattern, and food security. According to the various projections by the IPCC, extreme heat events are likely to be longer and more intense in addition to changes in precipitation patterns. The change in climate could: (a) affect the production of wheat, rice, and maize in the tropical and temperate zones, (b) have negative impact on health by exacerbating health problems that already exist especially in developing countries and (c) adversely impact productive activities like growing food and working outdoors.

9.2 Perceived Consequences of Climate Change

Changes observed in the Fourth Assessment Report of IPCC include: (a) shrinkage of glaciers, (b) thawing of permafrost, (c) lengthening of mid-to-high latitude growing seasons, (d) poleward and altitudinal shifts of plant and animal ranges, (e) decline in population of some plants and animals, (f) earlier flowering of trees and (g) changes in emergence of insects, and egg-laying in birds. Associations between changes in regional temperatures and the observed changes in physical and biological systems have been documented in many aquatic, terrestrial, and marine environments.

Changing environmental attributes are sure to affect the species spectrum and depending upon the pace of change, the profile and composition of forests is also likely to change. In arid or semi-arid areas, productivity is expected to decrease. Trends of drying up of wetlands and degradation of ecosystems have been observed.

The water cycle is totally dependent on the temperature regime. Increasing global temperature and resultant faster retreat of most glaciers is expected to affect the snow-fed perennial water regimes. Accordingly, the vegetation status of catchments, magnitude and frequency of floods, precipitation, run-off and groundwater recharge may be affected. It may substantially affect hydropower generation and increase in irrigation withdrawal, due to higher crop evaporative demand.

Changes in the frequencies of extreme heat and cold, the frequencies of floods and droughts, and the profile of local air pollution may result in changes in occurrence of infectious diseases, leading to impaired child development and various health consequences of population displacement and economic disruption.

Estimates of crop yield responses to climate change vary widely, depending upon species, cultivation practices, soil properties, and direct effects of carbon dioxide (CO_2) on plants. Even though increased CO_2 concentration can stimulate crop growth and yield that benefit may not always overcome the adverse effects of excessive heat and drought.

In countries with predominantly agrarian economies, increase in temperature and reduction in precipitation could—in the absence of adequate irrigation and related infrastructural interventions—dampen the economic growth by reducing agricultural productivity. These impacts can be moderated by efforts at adaptation but these are expected to be costly and will impose a burden on both producers and consumers.

For South Asia, warming has been predicted to be above the global mean and in South East Asia, equal to the global mean. Precipitation is likely to increase and extreme rainfall and other climatic events may occur more frequently. For India, extreme rains in South West monsoon and fewer rainy days along East Coast have been predicted.

For India and China, risks of dengue fever have been predicted by IPCC. Increase in flooding is associated with increased risk of drowning, diarrhoeal and respiratory diseases, and hunger and malnutrition.

9.3 United Nations Framework Convention on Climate Change (UNFCCC)

Recognizing the problem and the need for international co-operation, the international community in 1992 established the UNFCCC which accepted the principle of *common but differentiated responsibility* between the industrialized countries and the developing countries.

The objective of UNFCCC is to achieve stabilization of greenhouse gas concentrations in the atmosphere at a level that would prevent dangerous anthropogenic interference with the climate system. The Convention enjoins Parties to communicate information about the implementation of the Convention, taking into account the common but differentiated responsibilities and respective capabilities and their specific regional and national development priorities, objectives and circumstances. Article 12 of the Convention relates to the communication of information pertaining to implementation in accordance with Article 4 (1) of the Convention, whereby each Party is required to communicate to the Conference of the Parties. The elements of information in the communication are provided in the context of national circumstances and include:

1. A national inventory of anthropogenic emissions by sources and removals by sinks of all greenhouse gases not controlled by the Montreal Protocol, to the extent its capacities permit, using comparable methodologies to be promoted and agreed upon by the Conference of Parties;
2. A general description of steps taken to implement the Convention including an assessment of impacts, vulnerability due to climate change and associated adaptation needs; and
3. Any other information that the Party considers relevant to the achievement of the objective of the Convention and suitable for inclusion in its communication, including, if feasible, material relevant for calculations of global emission trends.

9.3.1 Kyoto Protocol: In 1997, parties signatory to UNFCCC adopted the Kyoto Protocol which set legally binding targets for GHG reductions by individual industrialized countries during *first commitment period, 2008-12*, totalling 5.2 percent below their aggregate 1990 emissions. The protocol did not involve any binding commitments by developing countries in recognition of the fact that historically it was the industrialized countries that were responsible for the overwhelming bulk of the stock of GHGs.

Kyoto Protocol made provisions for use of any of the three mechanisms including the Clean Development Mechanism (CDM) to help developed countries meet their quantified emission limitation and reduction commitments domestically and through acquisition of greenhouse gas reduction credits from activities outside their own boundaries at relatively lesser costs. India is a major participant in the projects aimed at using Clean Development Mechanism.

Kyoto Protocol took a more *top-down* but highly differentiated approach, establishing negotiated, binding emissions targets for developed countries, and no new commitments for developing countries.

175 countries including India ratified the Protocol. The US and some other countries did not ratify the Protocol. As it happens, most of those that did ratify the protocol have failed to live up to the commitments they had undertaken.

Under the provisions of the Kyoto Protocol, India as a non-annex I party, is not obliged to reduce emission of GHG. Under the Asia-Pacific Partnership on Clean Development and Climate, India has also been working with the US, Australia, China, Japan and Republic of Korea on possible development and promotion of clean technologies for dealing with climate change.

Kyoto Protocol came to an end in 2012.

9.3.2 Copenhagen Accord, 2009 and Cancún Agreements, 2010: With the Copenhagen Accord and Cancún Agreements, parties established a parallel *bottom-up* framework, with countries undertaking national pledges for 2020 that represented political rather than legal commitments. This approach attracted much wider participation, including, for the first time, specific mitigation pledges by developing countries. However, countries' pledges fell far short of the reductions needed to meet the goal set in Copenhagen and Cancún of keeping average warming below 2 degrees Celsius above pre-industrial levels.

9.3.3 Paris Agreement, 2015: The negotiations toward a Paris agreement were launched with the Durban Platform for Enhanced Action adopted at Seventeenth Conference of Parties (COP 17) in 2011. The Durban Platform called for *a protocol, another legal instrument or an agreed outcome with legal force under the Convention applicable to all Parties*, to apply from 2020, but provided no further substantive guidance.

COP 19 in Warsaw called on parties to submit *intended nationally determined contributions* (INDCs) well before the Paris conference, signalling an important bottom-up feature of the emerging agreement. Heading into Paris, more than 180 countries producing more than 90 percent of global emissions had submitted INDCs, a much broader response than many had anticipated.

The Paris Agreement marks the latest step in the evolution of the UN climate change regime, which originated in 1992 with the adoption of the Framework Convention. The UNFCCC established a long-term objective, general principles, common and differentiated commitments, and a basic governance structure, including an annual Conference of Parties (COP).

The U.N. Climate Change Conference in Paris (November 30 to December 12, 2015) presented a critical opportunity for parties to the U.N. Framework Convention on Climate Change (UNFCCC) to strengthen the global response to climate change. The negotiating mandate for the Paris talks called for a post-2020 climate agreement under the UNFCCC *with legal force* and *applicable to all Parties*. In fulfilling this mandate, the Paris conference was asked to produce a package: a core legal agreement and related instruments and decisions.

Parties to the UNFCCC reached a landmark agreement on December 12, 2015 in Paris, charting a fundamentally new course in the two-decade-old global climate effort.

Culminating a four-year negotiating round, the new treaty

ended the strict differentiation between developed and developing countries that characterized earlier efforts, replacing it with a common framework that commits all countries to put forward their best efforts and to strengthen them in the years ahead. This included, for the first time, requirements that all parties report regularly on their emissions and implementation efforts, and undergo international review.

A. Highlights of Paris Agreement: The agreement and a companion decision by parties were the key outcomes of the conference, known as the 21st session of the UNFCCC Conference of the Parties (or COP 21). The Paris Agreement:

1. Reaffirmed the goal of limiting global temperature increase well below 2 degrees Celsius, while urging efforts to limit the increase to 1.5 degrees.
2. Established binding commitments by all parties to make *nationally determined contributions* (NDCs), and to pursue domestic measures aimed at achieving them.
3. Committed all countries to report regularly on their emissions and *progress made in implementing and achieving* their NDCs, and to undergo international review.
4. Committed all countries to submit new NDCs every five years, with the clear expectation that they will *represent a progression* beyond previous ones.
5. Reaffirmed the binding obligations of developed countries under the UNFCCC to support the efforts of developing countries, while for the first time encouraging voluntary contributions by developing countries too.
6. Extended the current goal of mobilizing US$ 100 billion a year in support by 2020 through 2025, with a new, higher goal to be set for the period after 2025.
7. Extended a mechanism to address *loss and damage* resulting from climate change, which explicitly will not *involve or provide a basis for any liability or compensation.*
8. Required parties engaging in international emissions trading to avoid *double counting.*

9. Called for a new mechanism, similar to the Clean Development Mechanism under the Kyoto Protocol, enabling emission reductions in one country to be counted toward another country's NDC.

The strong momentum toward an agreement that built over the preceding months was dramatically underscored on the opening day of the summit by the presence of 150 presidents and prime ministers, the largest ever single-day gathering of heads of state. Impetus came also from a vast array of *non-state actors*, including governors, mayors and CEOs, and the launch in Paris of major initiatives like the Breakthrough Energy Coalition announced by Bill Gates and other billionaires.

Negotiations on many issues were hard-fought and, in typical COP fashion, progress through most of the conference was painstakingly slow. But thanks to deft diplomacy by the French presidency, the summit was remarkably free of the kind of procedural showdowns that marred previous COPs.

Many operational details of the new framework were left to be decided by future COPs. The agreement will take effect only once enough countries have formally ratified it.

9.4 Impact of Climate Change on India

India has always been subject to a large degree of climate variability. This is likely to be accentuated by climate change. Warming trends along the west coast, in central India, the interior peninsula, and north-eastern India and cooling trends in north-west India and parts of south India have been observed. Coasts are projected to be exposed to increase in risk including coastal erosion due to climate change and sea level rise. Geological Survey of India (GSI) projects that the glaciers of Himalaya are receding at varying rates in different regions.

9.4.1 Climate Change and Human Settlements: Climate change causes vulnerability of human settlements which is related to extreme weather events and such gradual changes in the climate exceed the adaptive capacity of human systems. Climate change adds to the existing stress on the sustainability of human settlements and society. Non-climate sources of change like rapid urbanisation are often the main source of stress.

Human settlements are accustomed to variability in environmental conditions and are resilient to normal variations. Vulnerabilities arise out of experiences that are beyond the normal experience and due to limited adaptive capacity. Climate change is likely to affect infrastructure related to water, sanitation, energy, transportation, healthcare, fire services and other forms of emergency measures.

The urban-heat island effects could get exacerbated due to increase in baseline temperatures, affecting climatic comfort of the urban populations and may consequently lead to additional costs in climate control.

Sustainable development concerns in the sense of enhancement of human well-being broadly conceived, are a recurring theme in India's development philosophy. The present day consensus reflects three foundational aspirations. *First that human beings should be able to enjoy a decent quality of life; second, that humanity should become capable of respecting the finiteness of the biosphere; and third, that neither the aspiration for the good life, nor the recognition of biophysical limits should preclude the search for greater justice in the world.* Sustainable habitat would mean achieving a balance between the economic and social development of human habitats together with the protection of the environment, equity in employment, shelter, basic services, social infrastructure and transportation. In the context of rapid urbanisation, there is wide awareness about the need to minimize the environmental costs of urbanisation. Environmental damage and depletion of non-renewable resources need to be addressed to meet present and future challenges such as climate change and associated vulnerabilities.

9.4.2 Climate Change and Water Supply: Climate change could affect water supply systems in any number of ways. It can affect the water demand for drinking and cooling systems. Where climate change leads to failure of small local water sources such as wells, it could lead to greater demand for regional water supplies. Changes in precipitation patterns could lead to reduction in water availability and fall in water tables. In coastal areas, it could lead to saline intrusions in rivers and ground water. Loss of melt water could reduce river flows during critical times.

A change in water availability and supply also affects sewered sanitation and drainage systems. When water supplies reduce, sewerage systems also become vulnerable. Further, sewage treatment plants are vulnerable to floods or sea level rise, as these are often located near rivers or seas. Where the sewer outfalls are in the sea, sea level rise will affect the functioning of such systems. Storm water drainage systems could become frequently overloaded and cause flooding if heavy storms become more frequent due to climate change. The impact of inadequate drainage systems in cities like Mumbai are already being felt leading to flooding and huge economic losses. More frequent floods could also present a significant threat if these lead to contamination of flood waters with faecal material.

9.4.3 Occurrence of Droughts: One of the climate change risks to the Indian economy and its people, and therefore to sustainability of habitats, is the increased intensity, frequency and geographical coverage of drought. Its primary impact is on rural areas where agriculture, animal husbandry, and to a lesser extent forestry and fishing, are significantly impacted leading to cycles of seasonal and distress migration. Droughts lead to drinking water shortages and increase in food and biomass fuel prices that hurt the urban poor and middle classes and hence the city economy. It also leads to a number of other impacts like depressed demand for secondary goods and services because of depressed agricultural demand. Climate change related impacts may render subsistence agriculture uneconomical in parts of semi-arid central, western and southern India, fuelling migration of rural population to urban areas.

Climate change may increase droughts in semi-arid peninsular and western India, leading to further misery for the landless and small and marginal farmers, who are typically forced to migrate to cities. They form the most vulnerable groups in cities—having limited skills, education, capital and access to social networks that underpin much economic and social mobility in urban India. They are also more likely to live in illegal and unserviced settlements that are exposed to a wide range of environmental risks varying from flooding to fire and continual cycles of demolition and eviction by civil authorities. They are therefore, dual victims of existing natural hazards and emerging climate change—displaced from their original places of residence and occupations and challenged by urban risks at their new places of residence.

9.4.4 River Hydrology and Inland Flooding: The most serious regional impact of climate change could be changes in the river hydrology in the Indo-Gangetic plain and the Brahmaputra valley due to glacial melt and regression of the Himalayan glaciers. The sustainability of habitats in these regions would be at risk. Inter-basin transfers could be amongst the options that might need to be considered.

Climate change is also expected to increase the severity of flooding in many Indian river basins, especially of the Godavari and Mahanadi along the eastern coast. Floods are expected to increase in north-western India adjoining Pakistan, and in most coastal plains in spite of existing upstream dams and multi-purpose projects. Extreme precipitation is expected to show a substantial increase in some parts of the country. Sanitation infrastructure is the main determinant of the contamination of urban flood-water with faecal material presenting a substantial threat of enteric diseases. In addition to flood hazards, more extreme rainfall events associated with climate change will also cause hazards from landslides in many urban centres in hilly regions.

Dealing with likely increase in risks associated with storm water will require a significant revision of urban planning practices across cities in the flood affected regions. Flood and climate change mitigation and adaptation measures will have to be integrated into day-to-day urban development and service delivery systems. Due to higher precipitation in more intense events, there is a need to increase the margin of design safety to enhance the hydraulic capacity of the sections. This will require additional investments.

9.4.5 Cyclonic Storms, Storm Surges and Coastal Flooding: Yet another important climate change induced risk is that of cyclonic storms, storm surges and accompanying coastal inundation. The high concentration of population, especially on the eastern coast, has led to extremely high vulnerability in this region, leading to devastating loss of life and property. The 1999 Orissa super cyclone killed over 10,000 people, devastated buildings, lifeline infrastructure and economic assets across 10 coastal and six inland districts, which included a number of towns and cities due to a mixture of devastating storm surges, cyclonic winds and coastal flooding.

Cyclones and storm surges could have a devastating impact on large urban centres including the mega cities of Mumbai and Chennai, the million plus cities of Vishakapatnam and Surat as well as other cities like Bharuch, Bhavnagar and Jamnagar apart from causing critical bottlenecks in important ports such as Kandla. Increased migration to the coast, powered by huge investments in coastal infrastructure, settlements and enterprises could lead to a substantial rise in losses.

9.4.6 Sea Level Rise: Rising sea levels in coastal areas would increase the risk of flooding and increase the vulnerability of communities residing in these areas, especially the poor.

It is estimated that sea level could rise by 3.5 to 34.6 inches between 1990 and 2100, making coastal groundwater saltier, endangering wetlands, and inundating valuable land and coastal communities. The most vulnerable stretches along the Western Indian coast are Khambhat and Kachchh in Gujarat, Mumbai and parts of the Konkan coast and south Kerala. The deltas of the Ganga, Krishna, Godavari, Cauvery and Mahanadi on the east coast may be threatened, along with irrigated land and a number of urban and other settlements that are situated in them. The loss of these important economic and cultural regions could have a considerable impact in some states.

There is also a need for better empirical data regarding storm surge and tidal gauge data for better appreciation of the impact of climate change in coastal areas. Tools like micro-modelling could help in developing better understanding.

According to Inter-Governmental Panel on Climate Change (IPCC), Indian coasts will be exposed to increasing risks such as coastal erosion due to climate change and sea level rise. Sea water intrusion is likely to increase the habitat of brackish water fisheries but coastal inundation is likely to damage the aquaculture industry significantly. Changes in currents, water temperature, salinity, strength of upwelling and mixing layer thickness in the West Pacific and North Indian Oceans are expected due to climate change.

Sea level rise will exacerbate the already declining fish productivity in Asia. Flooding caused by sea level rise is expected to affect millions of additional people, with small islands and the crowded delta regions around large Asian rivers (such as the Ganges and Brahmaputra) facing the highest risk. The IPCC has identified four deltas along the coast of India that are particularly vulnerable: Ganges-Brahmaputra (extremely vulnerable), Godavari (highly vulnerable), Krishna and Mahanadi (medium vulnerability). Stability of wetlands including mangroves and coral reefs around Asia is likely to be increasingly threatened.

9.5 India's Approach to Climate Change

The climate of India may be broadly described as tropical monsoonal type. India's climate is affected by two seasonal winds: the North-East monsoon and the South-West monsoon. The North-East monsoon, commonly known as the winter monsoon blows from land to sea, whereas the South-West monsoon, known as the summer monsoon blows from sea to land after crossing the Indian Ocean, the Arabian Sea, and the Bay of Bengal. The South-West monsoon brings most of the rainfall during a year in the country.

India is a large developing country with nearly 700 million rural population directly dependent on climate-sensitive sectors (agriculture, forests and fisheries) and natural resources (water, biodiversity, mangroves, coastal zones, grasslands) for subsistence and livelihoods. Further, the adaptive capacity of dry land farmers, forest dwellers, fisher folk and nomadic shepherds is very low.

Climate change may alter the distribution and quality of India's natural resources and adversely affect the livelihoods of its people. With an economy closely linked to its natural resource base and climatically-sensitive sectors, India may face a major threat because of the projected change in climate. With climate change, there would be increasing scarcity of water, reduction in yields of forest biomass, and increased risk to human health. The contribution of India to the cumulative global emissions is only 5 percent. Thus, historically and at present, India's share in the carbon stock in the atmosphere is relatively miniscule when compared to its distribution over the nation's population.

Climate change, resulting from anthropogenic emissions and increasing concentrations of a suite of gases called *green house gases* (GHGs)—mainly due to fossil fuel use, certain agricultural and industrial activities,. and deforestation—has the potential, over the next few generations, to significantly alter global climatic conditions. This would result in large changes in ecosystems, leading to possibly catastrophic disruptions of livelihoods, economic activity, living conditions, and human health. On the other hand, the abatement of GHGs involves significant economic costs.

While climate change is a global environmental issue, different countries bear different levels of responsibility for increases in atmospheric GHG concentrations. Further, the adverse impacts of climate change will fall disproportionately on those who have the least responsibility for causing the problem, in particular, developing countries including India.

Though India is a signatory to UNFCCC, it is not required to contain its GHG emissions. India's policies for sustainable development—by way of promoting energy efficiency and the use of renewable energy, changing the fuel mix to cleaner sources, energy pricing, pollution abatement, afforestation, mass transport—themselves result in a relatively GHG benign growth path.

9.6 National Action Plan on Climate Change (NAPCC)

As a part of voluntary actions to address climate change related concerns, India launched NAPCC on June 30, 2008. It stresses that maintaining a high growth rate is essential for increasing living standards of the vast majority of people of India and reducing their vulnerability of the impacts of climate change. Accordingly, it identifies measures that promote the objectives of sustainable development of India while also yielding to benefits for addressing climate change.

NAPCC estimated the per capita emissions of carbon dioxide in India at 1.02 metric ton per capita which is well below the world average of 4.25 and that for China at 3.60. The energy intensity of the economy is also demonstrated as having declined very considerably since the 1980s, to the present level comparing favourably with that of the least energy-intensive developed countries.

NAPCC is co-ordinated by the Ministry of Environment and Forests and implemented through the nodal Ministries and is aimed at advancing relevant actions in specific sectors/areas.

NAPCC advocates a strategy that promotes, firstly, the adaptation to climate change and secondly, further enhancement of the ecological sustainability of India's development path.

Eight National Missions—in the areas of solar energy, enhanced energy efficiency, sustainable agriculture, sustainable habitat, water, Himalayan ecosystem, increasing the forest cover, and strategic knowledge for climate change—form the core of

NAPCC. These National Missions represent multi-pronged, long-term and integrated strategies for achieving key goals in the context of climate change. The focus is on promoting understanding of climate change, adaptation and mitigation, energy efficiency and natural resource conservation.

State Governments are also preparing, under the advice of the Central Government, State Action Plans aimed at creating institutional and programme-oriented capacities to address climate change. These, together with the National Missions, will enhance climate change-related actions in the public and private domains.

The eight National Missions of NAPCC are as under:

1. Jawaharlal Nehru National Solar Mission (JNNSM).
2. National Mission for Enhanced Energy Efficiency (NMEEE).
3. National Mission on Strategic Knowledge for Climate Change (NMSKCC).
4. National Mission for Sustaining Himalayan Ecosystem (NMSHE).
5. National Water Mission (NWM).
6. Green India Mission (GIM).
7. National Mission on Sustainable Habitat (NMSH).
8. National Mission for Sustainable Agriculture (NMSA).

9.7 Prime Minister's Council on Climate Change

Government of India set up an elaborate institutional mechanism to consider and address issues relating to climate change. A Council chaired by Prime Minister called Prime Minister's Council on Climate Change was constituted in June 2007 to coordinate national action for assessment, adaptation and mitigation of climate change. The Council provides the overall guidance to climate change related actions taken by various Ministries of the Government and other agencies. The Council was reconstituted in November 2014 with the following objectives:

1. Co-ordinate national action plans for assessment,

adaptation and mitigation of climate change.

2. Advise government on pro-active measures that can be taken by India to deal with the challenge of climate change.
3. Facilitate inter-ministerial coordination and guide policy in relevant areas.

To sum up, India is conscious of the challenges of climate change and has implemented several major programmes addressing the climate variability concerns. These include: (a) cyclone warning and protection, (b) coastal protection, (c) floods and drought control and relief, (d) major and minor irrigation projects, (e) control of malaria, (f) food security measures and (g) research on drought resistant crops.

Climate change needs to be accounted as one of the potential risk factors affecting the outcome of any development programme or process in the long-run. Specific institutional arrangements are needed within government to oversee and monitor development in the context of the above necessities.

Forecasting systems and adaptations in response to climate change will be the key concerns for future development. For living systems, study of the impact of factors considered subject to rapid changes and their adaptation potential against the changing factors will be important. For predictions and early warning systems, understanding of the processes which could show discernible changes well before the actual impact starts is essential.

Vulnerabilities of India to climate change—in particular impacts on water resources, forests, coastal areas, agriculture, and health—should be identified. For this, co-ordinated efforts through the relevant scientific institutions, in both government and non-government sectors, are required. For specific thematic areas, nodal institutions can be identified and designated.

10

Agricultural Exports and Imports

Exports have acquired added significance in the wake of liberalization wave sweeping across the world. The trend towards market economy in almost all the countries of the world has increased the role of exports in developmental efforts. Exports have become an important indicator of a country's economic performance.

10.1 Agricultural Exports

Marine products, rice, wheat, sugar, oil meals, tea, coffee, cashew and spices are the prominent products of India's agriculture exports. Meat and meat preparations, fruits and vegetables and processed fruits and vegetables have recently shown strong growth. Despite the advantage of diverse agro-climatic conditions, enabling production of a great variety of products in various seasons, India's exports potential has not yet been adequately addressed. Main reasons for this are the following.

1. Poor export infrastructure.
2. Low level of agriculture product grading.
3. Lack of quality control.
4. Poor branding and packaging.

Infrastructure specific to agriculture exports such as storage, and fast track inland and mechanical port handling facilities are also limiting factors.

Almost all agricultural products are allowed to be freely exported. Export restrictions were removed on groundnut oil, agricultural seeds, wheat and wheat products, butter, rice and pulses from April 2002. Formation of exclusive agriculture export zones is an important step taken to focus on agriculture diversification, value addition and exports.

Export-Import (EXIM) Policy 2002-07 emphasized the importance of agricultural exports and announced the following policy measures to boost them.

1. Free exportability of all agricultural products except onions and niger seeds, exports of which are canalized through approved agencies.
2. Removal of procedural restrictions like requirement for registration, packaging etc.
3. Setting up of Agriculture Export Zones to enhance international market access and improve infrastructure facilities, and ensure better flow of credit.
4. Assistance for reducing the marketing costs such as transportation, handling and processing of export of selected agricultural commodities.
5. Financial assistance for improved packaging, strengthening of quality control mechanism and modernization of processing units.
6. Arranging promotion campaign such as buyer-seller meets and participation in important international fairs and exhibition.

10.1.1 Agriculture-export Zones (AEZs): In the Export-Import (EXIM) Policy 2002-07, Government announced the proposal to set up AEZs for the purpose of developing and sourcing raw materials and their processing/packaging leading to final exports. The underlying objective is to promote agricultural exports from the country and ensure remunerative returns to the farming community in a sustained manner.

The concept essentially embodies a cluster approach of identifying the potential products and the geographical region in which such products are grown and adoption of an end-to-end approach of integration of the entire process, right from the stage of production to consumption.

Under the scheme, the State Governments identify products with export potential which have comparative advantage in local production. State Government evolve a comprehensive package of services provided by all State

Government agencies, State agriculture universities and all institutions and agencies of the Central Government for intensive delivery in these zones. Corporate entities with proven credentials are also encouraged to sponsor new AEZs or take over already notified AEZs or part of such zones for boosting agriculture exports from the zones.

Services which are managed and co-ordinated by State Government/corporate sector include provision of pre- and post-harvest treatment and operations, plant protection, processing, packaging, storage and related research and development etc. Units in AEZs are entitled for all the facilities available for exports of goods in terms of provisions of the respective schemes. Agricultural and Processed Food Products Export Development Authority (APEDA) is the nodal agency of the Central Government to promote setting up of AEZs.

A web-based monitoring system has been evolved to monitor more than 120 activities in each AEZ. Under this monitoring system, each activity is defined, the agency responsible for undertaking the activity is indicated and the time for performing that activity is specified.

The benefits under Export Promotion Capital Goods Scheme, which were hitherto available only to direct exporters, have now been extended to service exporters in the AEZs. Thus, even service provided to ultimate exporters is eligible for import of capital goods at a concessional duty for setting up of common facilities. They fulfil their export obligation through receipt of foreign exchange from ultimate exporters who make the payments from their exchange earners' foreign currency (EEFC) account.

Exporters of value added agriculture products are eligible for sourcing duty-free fuel for generation of power, provided the cost component of power in the ultimate product is 10 percent or more and the input-output norms are fixed by the advance licensing committee of the DGFT. In view of the power-intensive nature of most of the value addition, almost all the exporters of value added agriculture produce are eligible for such facility.

Anticipated benefits of AEZs include the following:

1. Strengthening of backward linkages with a market oriented approach.
2. Product acceptability and its competitiveness abroad as well as in the domestic market.
3. Value addition to basic agricultural produce.
4. Bringing down cost of production through economy of scale.
5. Better price for agricultural produce.
6. Improvement in product quality and packaging.
7. Promoting trade-related research and development.
8. Increasing employment opportunities.

A. AEZs and NABARD: At present, Agricultural and Processed Food Products Export Development Authority (APEDA) has set up 60 Agri-Export Zones (AEZs) spread over 230 districts in 20 states. The crops covered include fruits, vegetables, spices, cashew, tea, basmati rice, medicinal plants, pulses etc. In all, 35 crops were identified for promotion in these zones.

NABARD initiatives in the promotion of AEZs are as under:

1. Keeping in view the larger objective of promoting exports, NABARD has extended 100 percent refinance scheme to all client institutions (CBs, RRBs, SCBs, SCARDBs with NPA not exceeding 5 percent). In order to augment the reach of bank credit and increase the production of commercial crops as also for creation of marketing avenues for the farmers, all contract farming arrangements (within and outside AEZs) are made eligible for availing special refinance package.
2. For accelerating the export growth of agricultural produce with institutional credit in AEZs, NABARD executed a tripartite agreement (MoU) with APEDA and EXIM Bank in November 2002 to synergise the efforts and to leverage

the respective strengths.

3. NABARD has provided a minimum repayment period of 3 years for all activities in AEZs.
4. Preparation of crop-specific credit plans for AEZs.
5. Sanctioned a scheme for cultivation and processing of Gherkins in Karnataka under co-financing scheme.

10.1.2 *Vishesh Krishi Upaj Yojana:* The objective of the scheme is to promote export of fruits, vegetables, flowers, minor forest produce, and their value added products, by incentivising exporters of such products.

A. Entitlement: Exporters of such products are entitled for duty credit scrip equivalent to 5 percent of the FoB value of exports for each licensing year commencing from April 1, 2004. The scrip and the items imported against it are freely transferable.

B. Imports Allowed: Duty credit may be used for import of inputs or goods including capital goods, as may be notified, provided the same is freely importable under ITC (HS). Imports from a port other than the port of export is allowed under Telegraphic Release Advice (TRA) facility as per the terms and conditions of the notification issued by the Department of Revenue.

C. Cenvat/Drawback: Additional customs duty/excise duty paid in cash or through debit under Vishesh Krishi Upaj Yojana is adjusted as Central Value Added Tax (CENVAT) credit or duty drawback as per rules framed by the Department of Revenue.

10.1.3 Agricultural and Processed Food Products Export Development Authority (APEDA): APEDA was established by the Government of India under the Agricultural and Processed Food Products Export Development Authority Act passed by the Parliament in December 1985. The Act came into effect from February 13, 1986 by a notification issued in the Gazette of India. The Authority replaced the Processed Food Export Promotion Council (PFEPC).

Headquartered in New Delhi, it is headed by a Chairman.

It has 5 regional offices in Guwahati, Hyderabad, Kolkata, Bangalore and Mumbai. It is entrusted with the task of promoting agricultural exports, including the export of processed foods in value added form. APEDA has also been entrusted with monitoring of export of 14 agricultural and processed food product groups listed in the Schedule to the APEDA Act. It is actively engaged in the development of markets besides upgradation of infrastructure and quality to promote the export of agro-products. In its endeavour to promote agro-products, APEDA provides financial assistance to the registered exporters under its schemes for: (a) market development, (b) infrastructure development, (c) quality development, (d) research and development and (e) transport assistance.

During 2009-10, APEDA was empowered by an Act of Parliament to enforce the intellectual property right (IPR) of geographical indications (GIs) for basmati rice.

A. Assigned Functions: In accordance with the Act of 1985, the following functions have been assigned to the Authority.

1. Development of industries relating to the scheduled products for export by way of providing financial assistance or otherwise for undertaking surveys and feasibility studies, participation in equity capital through joint ventures and other reliefs and subsidy schemes.
2. Registration of persons as exporters of the scheduled products on payment of such fees as may be prescribed.
3. Fixing of standards and specifications for scheduled products for the purpose of exports.
4. Carrying out inspection of meat and meat products in slaughter houses, processing plants, storage premises, conveyances or other places where such products are kept or handled for the purpose of ensuring the quality of such products.
5. Improvement of packaging of the scheduled products.
6. Improvement of marketing of the scheduled products outside India.

7. Promotion of export-oriented production and development of the scheduled products.
8. Collection of statistics from the owners of factories or establishments engaged in the production, processing, packaging, marketing or export of the scheduled products or from such other persons as may be prescribed on any matter relating to the scheduled products and publication of the statistics so collected or of any portions thereof or extracts therefrom.
9. Training in various aspects of the industries connected with the scheduled products.
10. Such other matters as may be prescribed.

B. Products Monitored: APEDA is mandated with the responsibility of export promotion and development of the following scheduled products:

1. Fruits, vegetables and their products.
2. Meat and meat products.
3. Poultry and poultry products.
4. Dairy products.
5. Confectionery, biscuits and bakery products.
6. Honey, jaggery and sugar products.
7. Cocoa and its products, chocolates of all kinds.
8. Alcoholic and non-alcoholic beverages.
9. Cereal and cereal products.
10. Groundnuts, peanuts and walnuts.
11. Pickles, papads and chutneys.
12. Guar gum.
13. Floriculture and floriculture products.
14. Herbal and medicinal plants.

In addition to this, APEDA has been entrusted with the responsibility to monitor import of sugar.

10.1.4 Strategy to Increase Agricultural Exports: In a country like India with 121 crore population and agriculture largely depending on the vagaries of monsoon, any strategy to promote agricultural exports will necessarily have demand and supply factors at its core, with instruments of procurement, storage and distribution to service the same. The periodic and recurrent spurts in the prices of essential commodities do not augur well for exports. It is, therefore, essential to have a clear policy about foodgrains based on the buffer norms and strict implementation of the same. As for the perishable products like fruits and vegetables, the country should have a system whereby critical reserves could be procured and stored at strategic locations by a centralized agency to ensure that any unusual rise in the price of a perishable essential commodity can be offsct by prompt delivery of sufficient quantities to control the prices. Such centrally procured stocks of perishable commodities if unutilised for price stabilization, can then be offloaded in the retail market or exported where possible with or without processing before the new harvest of that product comes into the market. This system will need to be fine-tuned to ensure availability of essential commodities at reasonable prices in the domestic market and at the same time continue with sustainable exports to remain a credible supplier in the international market.

A. Infrastructure and Technology: This kind of centralized procurement and storage will require substantial infrastructure to be built in terms of warehouses, cold storage, reefer vans, food processing plants with provision to press in service special railway rakes for swift distribution in the domestic market and shipment to the exporting ports. Dry port facilities may be created at strategic locations in the growing/processing areas to avoid any delays in handling procedures and pre-shipment inspections etc.

Appropriate schemes can be devised for providing incentives for warehousing in the private sector while Government can create the required infrastructure by going in for common facilities for packaging, creating corridors for perishable commodities and cargo handling centres for perishable commodities at all the airports and seaports.

B. Food Processing and Value Addition: Food processing and value addition will be crucial for any strategy to boost exports of agricultural products.

There is lot of wastage for want of post-harvest and food processing technology. Encouraging development of post-harvest technology and incentivising food processing in the producing areas should be central to any sustainable strategy to boost export of agricultural products from the country. Appropriate schemes can be devised to offer incentives for setting up food processing units in the rural areas which should not only generate employment but also provide platform for value addition and diversification of food products to meet the standards and requirements of the importing countries.

C. Market and Product Development: Any international trade in agricultural and processed food products depends on the international demand and supply situation, availability of the concerned product in the domestic market at reasonable price, health safety and quality standards as may be applicable in the importing countries and price competitiveness. For these reasons, it is important to disseminate information about the quality requirements of major markets, create a network of certifying agencies backed with laboratories manned by trained technicians. Besides, agreements for conformity of standards, standard equivalence and agriculture market access for agricultural products in the focus countries should be encouraged.

India is the home of spices and no other country in the world produces, consumes and exports spices in varied forms and in large volume as India does. The strategy in the spices sector aims at making India the premier supplier of quality spices, spice products and herbs in the global market. The medicinal and nutritional values of tea, coffee and spices should be studied and authenticated through clinical trials and patented for aggressive marketing.

10.2 Agricultural Imports

In recent years, edible oil, accounting for nearly 60 to 65 percent of the value of total agriculture imports, has become the single largest import item. Raw cashew, nuts (almonds from US) and pulses are among the other dominant agriculture imports. Of late, the share of agriculture imports in total imports of the country has hovered around 4 to 5 percent.

10.2.1 Protecting Domestic Agriculture: Lifting of quantitative restrictions on imports since April 2000 has resulted in import of a number of agriculture products which include fruits, juices, ketchups, meat products etc. Monitoring of 300 sensitive product imports has so far revealed that such imports are limited and, in the aggregate, constitute a small proportion of total agriculture imports. Contrary to concerns in some circles that liberalization of imports—resulting from the lifting of quantitative restrictions on agriculture products—would lead to surge of agriculture imports affecting adversely the Indian farmers, the value of agriculture imports in aggregate terms is quite low. India has considerable flexibility to counter flooding of the Indian market by cheap agriculture imports through imposition of tariffs (bound rate) under WTO. WTO permissible tariff rates are reasonably high as compared to actual rates. This should provide a fair level of protection. Countervailing duties can also be imposed to counter questionable subsidies given to agriculture products by the exporting countries apart from having the option of acting under safeguard provisions to counter surge of imports.

11

Indian Agriculture and World Trade Organization (WTO)

WTO is the only international body dealing with the rules of trade between nations. At its heart are the WTO agreements, the legal ground rules for international commerce and for trade policy. The agreements have three main objectives: (a) to help trade flow as freely as possible, (b) to achieve further liberalisation gradually through negotiations and (c) to set up an impartial means of settling disputes.

A number of simple, fundamental principles run throughout all the WTO agreements. They are the foundation of the multilateral trading system. They include: non-discrimination, freer trade, predictable policies, encouragement to competition and extra provisions for less developed countries.

The economic case for an open trading system based on multilaterally agreed rules is simple enough and rests largely on commercial common sense. Protectionism leads to bloated inefficient companies and can in the end lead to factory closures and job losses. One of the WTO's objectives is to reduce protectionism.

11.1 WTO in Brief

Created by Uruguay Round of Negotiations (1986-94), WTO was established on January 1, 1995 with headquarters in Geneva, Switzerland. Since July 29, 2016, 164 countries of the world are members of the WTO. WTO's creation in 1995 marked the biggest reform of international trade since 1948. During those 47 years, international commerce was regulated under General Agreement on Tariffs and Trade (GATT) which helped establish a prosperous multilateral trading system.

However, by the end of 1980s an overhaul was due.

The Eighth Round of multilateral trade negotiations held under GATT and named Uruguay Round, resulted in new legal agreements for trade and strengthening settlement system. Following this, there was a Ministerial Conference in Marrakesh, Morocco in April 1994 attended by 125 government representatives from across the world to sign for the establishment of a new successor institution of GATT, namely the World Trade Organization (WTO). WTO entered into force on January 1, 1995, with all assets and liabilities of GATT transferred to the former. WTO replaced GATT which remained in existence from 1948 to 1994. GATT was a multilateral treaty, governing trade in goods only. WTO is much wider in scope and coverage.

The Uruguay Round was the largest trade negotiations ever. At times the talks seemed doomed to fail, but in the end the Uruguay Round was successful. The task was so immense that some people wondered whether there would ever be another negotiations like these. Was it the round to end all rounds?

WTO is GATT plus a lot more. GATT (the institution) was small and provisional, and not even recognised in law as international organisation. It was replaced by WTO. GATT (the agreement) was amended and incorporated into the new WTO Agreements. GATT dealt only with trade in goods. WTO Agreements cover services and intellectual property as well.

Broadly speaking, WTO has set to continue negotiations and bring agreements in the following areas.

1. Basic telecommunications.
2. Maritime transport.
3. Movement of natural persons.
4. Financial services.
5. General Agreement on Trade and Services (GATS).
6. A reaffirmation of the rule of law in trade and economic relations.
7. A reversal of long standing protectionist practices in

agriculture, textiles and clothing.

8. An extension of multilateral rules to services and intellectual property rights.

WTO is run by its member governments. All major decisions are made by the membership as a whole, either by ministers (who meet every two years) or by officials (who meet regularly in Geneva). Decisions are normally taken by consensus. More routine work is supervised by the General Council. Numerous other councils, committees, working parties and negotiating groups cover the wide range of WTO issues.

WTO is directed by a Ministerial Conference which is the highest authority and meets at least once every two years. So far, Ministerial Conferences have been held in Singapore (December 1996), Geneva (May 1998), Seattle (November-December 1999), Doha (November 2001), Cancun (September 2003), Hong Kong (December 2005), Geneva (November-December 2009), Geneva (December 2011), Bali (December 2013 and Nairobi (December 2015).

WTO is based on the principles of non-discrimination, free trade and promotion of fair competition among the member countries. About 95 percent of the global trade is governed by the rules and regulations of WTO.

WTO agreements are permanent and ratified by the Parliaments of member countries.

11.2 Agreements on Agriculture at WTO

11.2.1 Agreement of Agriculture (AoA): AoA of WTO recognises free and market-oriented trading system in agriculture. It has the following main features.

A. Tariffication: It means conversion of all non-tariff barriers on trade such as import quota into tariffs. Tariff bindings are to be reduced under this agreement. (A tariff binding is a commitment not to exceed a particular level of tariff). Developed countries were to reduce their tariff bindings over a period of six years (1995-2000). Developing countries are to reduce their bindings over a period of ten years (1995-2004). Least developed countries are exempted from tariff reductions.

B. Market Access: Where tariff bindings are too high, current market access has to be maintained as the amount of exports to other countries at preferential tariff rates. However, market access provisions do not apply when the commodity in question is a traditional staple in the diet of a developing country.

C. Domestic Support: WTO member countries are subject to following obligations on domestic support to their agriculture.

11.2.2 Aggregate Measure of Support (AMS): It is the annual level of support in monetary terms extended to agricultural sector. It is the non-exempted support of the following two types: (a) product-specific support, i.e. market price support/subsidy given to the producer of a specific crop. (b) non-product specific support, i.e. total of subsidies on inputs like power, irrigation, fertilizers and credit. The AMS is calculated for each product receiving market support and is based on the price prevailing in the base period (1986-88). If AMS exceeds 5 percent of the total value of agricultural production in the case of developed countries (10 percent for developing countries), these are to be reduced by 20 percent over six years from 1995 (13.3 percent over ten years for developing countries). The AMS to Indian agriculture is still below 10 percent in terms of WTO stipulations.

However, there are many issues under the AoA which are considered against the interests of developing countries like India.

Firstly, the minimum access for import of primary goods flouts the basic rule of promoting free trade under WTO agreement. The *blue box* and *green box* subsidies are exempted from reduction commitments, leading to distortion in trade. This has been emphasized by developing countries like India which have a majority of low cost agricultural producers.

Secondly, distortions emerge from inequity in domestic subsidy discipline due to different base positions. The developed countries are heavily subsidized countries and are allowed to retain up to 80 percent of their subsidies but developing countries can subsidise their farmers not more than 10 percent of the total value of agricultural production. Hence, the domestic support by developed countries needs to be reduced substantially in absolute terms.

Thirdly, the domestic support measures relaxed for the purpose of food security and PDS are allowed only in relation to the international market price and to the targeted population. However, this creates problem for countries like India with high percentage of poor population and heavy dependency on agriculture. Food security which is interlinked with the livelihood security is extremely important for densely populated countries with a large agrarian economy. These countries need enough flexibility under the AoA to take care of their food security, rural employment and livelihood concerns.

Fourthly, India has argued that for low income countries, market access and domestic support discipline should be such that their food requirements are met from domestic sources. The volatile international market can get transmitted to the domestic economy and can affect the prices of foodgrains and food entitlement of the poor. Hence, it was suggested that for development of agriculture in developing countries, diversification of *green box* subsidies should be encouraged and input subsidies allowed to crops where productivity levels are below the world average. Also, the negative product-specific support may be permitted so as to be adjusted against non-product-specific support..

Fifthly, developing countries face highest tariff rates which include the major agricultural staple foods, cereals, meat, sugar, milk, butter, cheese as well as tobacco products and cotton. A study conducted by WTO with United Nations Conference on Trade and Development (UNCTAD) suggests that tariff wedge will continue to be significantly high on account of tariff escalation which is a major factor preventing developing countries from diversifying and increasing their share of processed agricultural exports.

The Indian proposals have, by and large, been well received

and endorsed by most of the developing countries as well as some of the developed countries. However, it is important that steps are taken to reap benefits of a liberalized trade regime through increased efficiency in agriculture and combat restrictions by developed countries arising from sanitary and phtyo-sanitary measures. Efficiency would be greatly enhanced with increased investment and land reforms. Also, diversification of agricultural production into agro-foods, horticulture and floriculture products and farm products with international quality standards could help to increase exports from this sector.

11.2.3 Green Box Support: It is given on items which have minimal impact on trade, e.g. pest and disease control, market intelligence, infrastructure services, relief from natural disaster, and buffer stock operations. It is an exempted support.

11.2.4 Blue Box Support: It is product-limiting subsidy and pertains mainly to the developed countries. It is exempted from reduction commitment under WTO. The developed countries subsidise their agriculture mainly under green and blue boxes.

11.2.5 Special and Differential Treatment Box Support: It includes investment subsidy to agricultural sector for farm development work like land levelling, shallow wells etc. It also includes agricultural input services to low-income and resource poor farmers. This support is mainly related to the developing countries and is exempted from reduction commitment under WTO.

11.2.6 Export Competition: WTO member countries are obliged to reduction commitments of their direct export subsidies. Developed countries are to reduce the volume of subsidised agricultural exports by 21 percent and the value of subsidies by 36 percent of the average base period 1986-88 within six years. Developing countries are to reduce the same by 14 percent and 24 percent respectively within ten years.

11.3 Special Safeguard Mechanism (SSM)

As regards tariffication, there is a misconception that India is reducing import duties on agricultural products under WTO compulsions. As a matter of fact, the actual import duties on a variety of agricultural products are lower than the tariffs (bound rates) under WTO.

SSM was a key issue in the Doha Development Agenda (DDA). SSM embodies the right to impose trade barriers if there is a surge in agricultural imports into India. In the Uruguay Round, many countries including India were allowed to set ceiling tariff bindings, i.e. they were allowed to set, as their WTO obligation, high levels of tariffs which range from 40 percent to 100 percent to 150 percent. In a preponderance of tariff lines, there is a considerable gap between applied tariffs and the level of tariff bindings. Once India had this freedom, it was not necessary to have safeguard actions because, in response to import surges, but even otherwise, India could raise tariffs up to the high level of bindings. In other words, the applied rates are lower than bound rates (Table 11.1).

Table 11.1: India's Actual and Bound Rates in Agriculture

(Percent)

Bound minus applied	No. of tariff lines	Cumulative tariff lines	Percentage	Cumulative
0	21	21	1.6	1.6
1-5	20	41	1.5	3.1
6-10	136	177	10.4	13.5
11-20	39	216	3.0	16.4
21-30	109	325	8.3	24.7
31-40	354	679	26.9	51.7
41-60	111	790	8.4	60.1
61-80	235	1,025	17.9	78.0
81-100	101	1,126	7.7	85.7
Above 100	188	1,314	14.3	100.0
Total	1,314			

Source: Government of India, Economic Survey, 2015-16, Volume I, Chapter 1, Table 2.

In the context of fears expressed in some quarters that liberalisation of imports would lead to surge of agricultural imports affecting Indian farmers adversely, the Economic Survey, 2001-02 observed, "India has considerable flexibility to counter flooding of the Indian market by cheap agriculture imports by imposing tariffs (bound rate) under WTO for agriculture products which provide a fair level of protection. The Government, in fact, raised the import tariff for many agriculture products such as tea, coffee, pulses and edible oils in the last budget (2001-02). Countervailing duties can also be imposed to counter actionable subsidies given to agriculture products by the exporting countries apart from having the option of acting under safeguard provisions to counter surge of imports". [1]

11.4 Agriculture at the Hong Kong Ministerial Conference of WTO

India is a founder member of WTO. It has taken active interest in the deliberations of WTO. In fact, India has emerged as the leading voice of the developing world at various rounds of trade negotiations.

At the Doha round of trade negotiations, Members adopted a Framework Agreement outlining the elements and principles which would guide further negotiations. The framework, detailed modalities and specific commitments of each Member in respect of Agriculture and Non-Agricultural Market Access (NAMA) were discussed at the Sixth Ministerial Conference of WTO held at Hong Kong, China in December 2005.

Negotiations on agriculture, which have been taking place in special sessions of the WTO Committee on Agriculture, focused on achieving progressive and substantial reforms in global agricultural trade. While the discussions leading to Cancun had centred around bridging the divergence between the common positions taken by the European Community (EC) and US and those of the G-20 alliance, post-Cancun deliberations strengthened the G-20 alliance and emphasized their outreach to others, in particular, the G-33 alliance of developing countries on Special Products, the Africa Group, and the Cairns Group of agricultural exporting countries. The G-20 was successful in exposing the EC-US as demandeurs of substantial market access in developing countries, in particular, the large and relatively more advanced among them, and without regard to their legitimate food and livelihood security and rural development concerns, with only minimal market access commitments being called forth from themselves.

The G-20 also emphasized the requirement to eliminate all forms of export subsidies within a credible timeframe and to achieve substantial reductions in trade-distorting domestic support. In the lead up to the WTO General Council Decision of August 1, 2004 (Framework Agreement), the negotiations among the Five Interested Parties (FIPs), comprising of EC, US, Australia, Brazil and India, resolved the divergent positions on key aspects of each of the three pillars in the agriculture negotiations.

The Framework Agreement explicitly agrees to eliminate export subsidies by a credible end date. It imposes a down payment of 20 percent on overall trade-distorting domestic support in the first year of implementation, besides containing a combination of cuts, disciplines and monitoring requirements in the various elements of the domestic support pillar, and a tiered formula for tariff reductions based on proportionately lower commitments by developing countries than by developed countries. The Framework also recognizes the critical importance of agriculture to the economic development of developing countries and the need to enable them to pursue agricultural policies that are supportive of their development goals, poverty reduction strategies, food security and livelihood concerns, including through instruments such as Special Products and a new Special Safeguard Mechanism against likely import surges. The Framework, thus, provides a useful basis for further negotiations on detailed modalities that could help create market access opportunities for products of export interest and safeguard small and vulnerable producers of farm products.

The Ministerial Declaration adopted at the end of the conference called for conclusion of negotiations launched at Doha, and established time-frames and targets in specific areas:

1. Resolve to complete the Doha Work Programme fully, and to conclude negotiations in 2006.
2. To establish modalities in agriculture and non-agricultural market access (NAMA) by April 30, 2006 and prepare draft Schedules by July 31, 2006.
3. To eliminate export subsidies in agriculture by 2013, with a substantial part in the first half of the implementation period. Developing countries without Aggregate Measurement of Support (AMS), such as India, will be exempt from reductions in *de minimis* and the overall cut in trade-distorting domestic support, consisting of AMS, the Blue Box and *de minimis*, that is entitlement to provide Amber Box subsidies up to 10 percent of value.
4. To submit a second round of revised services' offers by July 31, 2006 and submit final draft schedules by October 31, 2006.
5. Amendment to TRIPS Agreement reaffirmed to address public health concerns of developing countries.
6. Duty-free, quota-free market access for all LDCs' products to all developed countries. Developing country declaring itself to be in a position to do so, to also provide such access, though flexibility in coverage and in the phase in of their commitments is provided.
7. In cotton, export subsidies to be eliminated by developed countries in 2006 and trade-distorting domestic subsidies to be reduced more ambitiously and over a shorter period of time.

11.5 India's Stand on Agricultural Issues

1. Substantial and effective reductions in overall trade-distorting domestic support (OTDS) of the US and EU.

2. Self-designation of an appropriate number of special products (SPs).
3. An operational and effective Special Safeguard Mechanism (SSM).
4. Simplification and capping of developed country tariffs.

To sum up, the post-Uruguay Round experience has been a mixed one for agricultural trade in India. In the ongoing negotiations on the Agreement on Agriculture, India submitted detailed proposals with a view to safeguarding the food and livelihood security of the large subsistence level farming community and maximising export opportunities for Indian agricultural products by seeking a reduction in the high tariffs and subsidies prevent in developed countries.

The Indian Parliament had passed the Protection of Plant Varieties and Farmers' Rights Act, 2001 with the objective of giving a significant thrust to agricultural growth by providing an effective system for the protection of plant varieties and farmers' rights. This is expected to stimulate investments for research and development both in the public and the private sectors for the development of new plant varieties by ensuring appropriate returns on such investment.

A higher growth in agriculture, thus, needs a comprehensive revamp of agriculture policy with reorientation towards rapid diversification of this sector. A progressive correction is required in the incentive structure for agriculture so that the excessively high minimum support prices do not continue to distort resource allocation in agriculture. This will ensure that farmers diversify towards high value added segments of agriculture in response to the new demand structure.

Endnote

1. Government of India, *Economic Survey,* 2001-02, p. 205.

Appendix

Appendix

Political Economy of Agriculture in Uttar Pradesh

Introduction

The state of Uttar Pradesh is one of the highly populated states in India. The report of the Census data 2011 states that, U.P.'s population has crossed over 166 million people. This percentage accounts for about 16.4 percent of the country's population and the land cover of the state stood at 7.5 percent of the country's geographical area.

The state of Uttar Pradesh, in geographical sense is a landlocked state, primarily rural with mainly an agrarian economy. The State's industrialization pattern is highly skewed, whereby the industries largely find their presence in the western region of the state. The major crops cultivated in the state are wheat, rice, sugarcane, pulses and vegetables, and the primary industries consist of cement, vegetable oils, textiles, cotton yarn, sugar, jute and carpet.

Gross state domestic product of Uttar Pradesh for the year 2010-11 consisted of a 33 percent share from agriculture, 24 percent from the industrial sector, 11 percent from the manufacturing, while the remaining 43 percent from the services sector.

Castes and Communities in Uttar Pradesh

The Hindus and the Muslims are the two primary important religious communities in the state of Uttar Pradesh, each of which is further sub-divided into castes and sub-castes.

The Muslim population constitutes about 16 percent of the State's total population. It is the presence of the communal conflict in the State that appears to be an important feature of state politics than that of caste conflicts, both during the colonial period and that of the years followed by Independence till today. For instance, a tradition of Hindu-Muslim conflict over issues such as Urdu or the position of the Aligarh Muslim University developed during the colonial period and continued thereafter.

The formation of Hindu Mahasabha worsened the situation. The compulsory sterilizations during the emergency period, the issue of Ram Janam Bhoomi and Babri Masjid have been few of the very sensitive and main issues in the recent past. These communal issues have managed to create greater bitterness and frequent conflicts.

Land System

Talukdari and Zamindari systems were the two important forms implemented by the British government in the United Provinces, to manage land revenue in the region. Joint zamindars and individual zamindars were formed to manage land revenues in the north-eastern region of the United Province, while the rights of revenue collections and ownership were given to talukdars in the Oudh.

This pattern of revenue collection and ownership gave rise to zamindari system and led to the skewed and concentrated land ownership and as a result, class and regional variation arose out of this system.

The bigger size of land ownership of zamindars and talukdars led to the extraction of both economic and political power in the areas under their control (this is one of the reference points where the political economy approach has been highlighted to understand politics and agricultural development in Uttar Pradesh).

According to the Zamindari Abolition Committee, "by Independence, 56 percent of the cultivators had a holding of less than 2 acres and shared among themselves, less than 15 percent of the land". According to the Agricultural Census of Uttar Pradesh in 1991, "eighty one percent of the total cultivators had 39 percent of the total land and the cultivating holdings of less than 5 acres each. Another 13 percent had holdings between 5 to 10 acres and cultivated 26 percent of the land, while remaining 6 percent possessed 35 percent of the total land.

One fourth of the land was under the possession of 3 percent of the cultivators with holdings of 14 acres or more". In central and eastern districts, prior to the land reforms, inequality in the sense of distribution of land ownership was much large. However, some of the work done on land distribution shows that the western region of the state did not see such kind of extreme polarization.

In the western area, land was fairly distributed with medium size land owners owning 5.25 acres and around 18 percent of the area and the next 13 percent owning farming land of 25 acres. [1]

The data collected by National Sample Survey of 1998-99 suggests that not much has changed. Therefore, it can be said that, land reforms have been unable to bring any institutional change in the pattern of cultivation. Land reforms were also unable to reduce disparity among different regions of the state; at best they only helped in removing absentee landlordism.

The 1995-96 Agricultural Census shows that the pattern of landholding remains skewed. It is found that, on an average, 73 percent held below one hectare of land in the state, of which the western region reflects 62 percent and it keeps on rising as one move towards the eastern region.

In central U.P. and the hill areas, it stood at about 70 percent and grows strikingly to a little above 80 percent in the plains of eastern U.P. Only in Bundelkhand, does it drop sharply to 47 percent. [2] Thus, we find that, large sized land holdings are present mainly in the Bundelkhand region, small size holdings are present in the eastern U.P., while the mid size land holdings are heavily concentrated in the western region and to a lesser dimension in the central region of the state of U.P. It is important to remember this land distribution pattern when studying the land holdings data with electoral and economic data.

Agrarian Classes

The government of Uttar Pradesh has been preparing and maintaining the statistical data on the land owning size since 1950s. It is important to classify and identify the major agrarian classes. According to the land owning pattern, the agricultural population in the state of Uttar Pradesh can be classified into five major classes.

- Big land owning class.
- Rich farmers.
- Mid level cultivators.
- Small land holders.
- Marginal farmers.

This classification of agrarian classes is based on the size of distribution of operational holdings and the labour involved and some non-qualified agrarian characteristics. Big land owning classes are found to own more than ten hectares of land.

This agrarian class often uses hired labour instead of the family labour; at times they also rent out the land to other cultivators and extract surplus in the form of rental agreement. Although many of them still use the pre-capitalist mode of extraction of surplus in agriculture, in some areas of the state, it is found that this big land owning class in the post economic reforms era (1991 onwards) have adopted newer technologies initiated by the Green Revolution to boost their agricultural production.

Rich farmers own somewhere around 4-10 hectares of land. They are a class of self-cultivating farmers and also many a times lease land for self-cultivation to raise their land holdings and income. Rich farmers use hired labour all around the year.

Studies from western U.P. show that rich farmers with larger holdings have begun to hire permanent farm servants who manage the farm and hire causal labour when required. A distinct feature of this class has emerged since the 1960s, and that is the adoption of the new agrarian technology by the rich farmers in the state. As a consequence of this, rich farmers have managed to gain advantage over the other middle level and small peasants. The middle and small cultivators have moved towards the new technology only recently. [3]

The reason for late adoption of new technology by mid level and small farmers has been the high costs of inputs, knowledge and technology and their respective availability. T.J. Byres, describes "rich farmers as those using both the bio-chemical and mechanical innovations of the technology". [4]

The rich farming class described above is similar in various forms to that of the "bullock capitalists" described by Rudolph and Rudolph. However, the study conducted by Rudolph and Rudolph does not differentiate between rich and mid level cultivating agrarian class. For them, "bullock capitalist means those who own 2.5-15 acres". [5]

Cultivators owning land share between one to two hectares constitute the class of small farmers, while the cultivators owning less than or below one hectare of land forms the class of marginal farmers in the state.

Most of them exist in the form of tenants and hiring outside labour is not an option for them. Therefore, it will be logical to suggest that these two classes largely form the class of agricultural labourers. In the structure of agrarian hierarchy, these two classes together form the poorest and lowest section and the mode of cultivation remains subsistence/primitive for them.

A pertinent observation suggests that these classes together constitute the largest section of agrarian classes (numerically). This fact bears importance in the study from the political-economic point of view.

As the implications of various agricultural policies is highest for this class, figures show the percentage of land held by each of these classes in the districts of U.P.

Green Revolution

It was the Green Revolution policy programme during 1960-1970 that brought high yielding varieties of wheat and rice in parts of western Uttar Pradesh, Haryana and Punjab. This, as a consequence, made India a food sufficient country from the food deficient one.

However, the land area under cultivation remained constant and it was with the higher use of fertilizers that made it possible to increase the yields, thereby extending the use of the available land to its maximum potential. Therefore, the increase in the yields of the fields under the Green Revolution policy in rural areas led to developmental and economic gains for the cultivators.

The new policies formulated for the agrarian sector focused at enhancing agricultural productivity, and these policies and programmes subsequently came to be known as the Green Revolution.

In the present discussion of these policy changes, the aim remains at understanding those factors, which are responsible for bringing alliance between the state and agrarian capitalism, and not taking implications of the Green Revolution policies in its distributional consequences.

It will be okay to say that Green Revolution policies and technologies draw a relationship in the revision of the primary political economy of India (a development-oriented nexus among varied political elite and the private enterprising class).

This different approach to agrarian sector represents "more of a clarification of priorities within the agrarian sector and less of a shift in inter-sectoral patterns of public investment". [6] Byers argues that during 1966-67, distribution of public expenditure funds did not see much sectional change rather the amount of funds allocated to agrarian sector remained the same and what changed was the nature of utilization.

Before adopting the new approach, it can be argued that the Indian state never had a routinized agricultural policy. The aim for agrarian sector was to improve production and ensure redistribution, as that for the rest of the economy.

However, the policies to reach these goals remained deficient. For instance, cooperative farming was encouraged along with community development programmes, land reforms, improvement in irrigation and agricultural extension services and so on. Unfortunately, these initiatives failed in achieving the goals of improving levels of agricultural productivity and its distribution.

Thus, it is clear that the aim of the new approach for agriculture was to increase agricultural production and adoption of those policy measures and technology, which will ensure in achieving this target.

Politics of Agrarian Mobilization

Mobilization of agrarian rural classes is of various types and caters to various agrarian classes and their issues. Historically, different patterns can be found in the case of India describing the changing pattern of agrarian demand politics and issues involved overtime.

During the British period, in the historically existing United Province, the big landlords were able to constitute associations/groups to protect their interests against the attempt of the British Empire to help tenants and also to put away demands by the poor cultivators and landless labourers. After 1947, efforts were made to protect landlords' interests by political mobilization.

However, it turned out to be unsuccessful and was reflected as the failure of the Praja Party in the elections of 1952, and most importantly its failure to block zamindari abolition policy. The Congress leadership attempted to avoid any class conflict and a clash with the zamindar class, and therefore paid the compensation.

However, it went forward with the Zamindari Abolition Act implementation. Therefore, by 1950s, the Congress government had become an electoral party which represented the interests of small landlord class, wealthy landowners and cultivators and under proprietors who defined themselves as to constitute the class called Bhumidars (owner-proprietor).

During the 1960s, the Swatantra Party made a brief and unsuccessful attempt to represent conservative land interests. However, bigger landowners individually still exercise considerable power in the rural areas and rely on social and family networks to put pressure on the bureaucracy, police and local political leaders to safeguard their interests.

It is worthy to note that, during the decade of 1970, various attempts were made by 'populist electoral parties' to mobilize small and marginal cultivators and landless tenants in order to address the issue of redistribution of land.

In recent years, the pursuit of commercial farming based on liberal market policy and profit maximization has led to the rise of a different way of agrarian mobilization. This mobilization of the newly formed rich peasantry class by farming is based on political parties and/or farmers movements in the state.

During the years of 1950s and 1960s, issues such as land reforms, taxation of agricultural income, trading of foodgrains and so on were the most debated ones. During the 1970s and 1980s, unremunerated rates for farm commodities along with the terms of trade with the industry constituted central issues under the agrarian policy.

The rise of Bhartiya Kisan Dal party in the state of U.P. in 1967 led to the mobilization of agrarian classes and not just the mobilization by farmer's organization, having acquired economic power as an outcome of the adoption of the new agrarian technology. The rich landlord farmer class, particularly under the leadership of Charan Singh, also aspired to gain political power. The rural-urban divide did not become an important factor in the definition of political economy of the state.

The pertinent issue to take note of is that, after the demise of Charan Singh, Bhartiya Kisan Union (BKU) under the new leadership of Mahendra Singh Tikait—primarily in the western U.P.—has emerged as a powerful non-party agrarian lobby influencing the politics of the state. Thereafter, followed a period which can be seen as a mobilization of agrarian rural classes by electoral parties, important in the state of U.P.

Politics and Agrarian Interests

Some important studies about the politics and agrarian

interests in the state of U.P. from mid-1960s reflect that there is a growing nexus between different rural agrarian classes and the state electoral. This is seen as an outcome of the implications of the state assembly elections that occurred in U.P. since 1969 onwards.

In the state of U.P., all-India political parties such as the Congress, Jan Sangh, Swatantra party, Janata Party and the communist parties have historically played many important roles. The BKD/LD had managed to gain enough base in the western region of U.P. and can be described as an important regional party, but the party was unable to gain power on its own and as a result has always formed alliance with non-Congress political forces. [7]

U.P. remains primarily a rural agrarian state and naturally all electoral parties were bound to come up with attractive agrarian programmes and form a rural agrarian base even if it is challenging to gain power. The peasant-based parties like BKD/LD have been a political-cum-farming interest group that represents the rich landlord peasantry.

The agrarian perspectives and priorities of the other political parties have shifted during these years. However, no political party today can bypass the political clout of the huge bunch of peasantry class and thus all of them have made various efforts to gain their support.

Congress Party: The state of Uttar Pradesh formed a reliable constituency of the Congress party during the freedom struggle and continued to be so in early 1950s. However, today the dominance of Congress party in U.P. (as per the results in the 2012 U.P. state assembly elections), and its strongly felt presence has come to be in doubt and serious questions have been raised to examine its decline.

It is evident that the ways of mobilization, support system and the base of the Congress party has undergone drastic changes over the years.

During the British colonial era and in the early years, the Congress was able to get the support of the big landholders along with the tenants and the small cultivators. This is primarily due to its composition of being a broad-based political party comprising of the conservatives, swarajists, socialists and others who were involved with the kisan sabhas.

In 1947, the Congress party appeared as a party that supported the interests of the small-size landholders and relatively bigger tenants in north India, specifically in U.P. This was due to the reason that for many years, its interests had come to align with this group and not with the big landlords or even the poorer landless peasantry.

This group provided the required support for the Congress party in U.P. during the 'no rent campaigns' and also in the civil disobedience movements organized by the Party. Congress party was against both the landlords holding huge areas of land and the British rule.

Stanley Kochanek's study of the Congress shows that in the 1930s, the rural gentry began to join the Party in large numbers. In fact, the generation of the thirties, which was caught up in the Gandhian movement was drawn predominantly from rural areas. As a result of such developments, the task of the Zamindari Abolition Committee has to be seen as one of sufficiently undermining the grade and status of the bigger landlords, while on the other hand contributing politically and economically to the strength of the smaller landholders and tenants. This is the group that had become the primary basis of the Congress electoral base in the rural country side.

Bhartiya Kranti Dal/Bhartiya Lok Dal: After the Congress party, the BKD or BLD as a political party came to have claimed grounds in the 1970s. It also emerged as one of the major political groups in the state of U.P. after mid-1960s. The BKD came into being after the 1967 elections when Charan Singh along with his followers broke away from the Janata Party in April 1967 and formed a new group earlier called the Jana Congress. The BKD came up as a party mainly confined to the state of U.P.

The BKD formed itself as one of the different anti-Congress groups during the mid-1960s. The BKD was different due to its distinct set of ideology.

The ideological path and nature of the party can be examined by taking a detailed look at the ideas, programs and writings of Charan Singh, the founding father of the party. The political activities of the party are well known including his books and articles (though they have not been given adequate importance). Charan Singh had spent about forty five years with the Congress organization.

While working with the Congress party, he managed to develop a different economic view point and a regional political representation. Charan Singh always supported the peasant proprietor and this could be noticed on various occasions prior to 1967.

Jan Sangh/Bhartiya Janata Party: The Jan Sangh is the sole political group in Northern India that did not emerge out of the Congress organization. Its U.P. unit is of importance because it was initiated in 1951 and succeeded to build itself into an important opposition party at least during early 1960s. In the following years, the party converted itself into another organization called the Bhartiya Janata Party, and eventually this party emerged as an important national party, in terms of its organizational structure, nature of work and ideology, which was very different from the rest of the parties in U.P.

Various studies done during the 1960s reflects that many of the Jan Sangh MLAs hailed from the upper elite castes, and were mainly urban-based although they came from a zamindari background. It for sure did not reflect the ideas of the rural landless poor or the lower castes.

Various studies argue that the Congress party had the representation of the upper castes as well as lower castes especially in rural areas. While on the other hand, the Jan Sangh organization reflected the interests of the upper and the middle class.

In fact, in the study done by Paul Brass, he suggests that, "the leadership and main electoral support of the party in the 1960s came largely from merchants, shopkeepers, and businessmen in the towns and big landlords in the rural areas". [8]

Janata Party: Janata Party was formed in 1977, and it had a particularly important bearing for the political economy of U.P. The Janata Party acquired power at the centre and in U.P. on two major platforms: (i) to bring the focus of economic activities from urban areas to the rural countryside and (ii) to free Indian politics of extreme degrees of centralization and authoritarian leadership.

At the Centre, the government followed new economic policies and programmes along with a Five Year Plan (1978-1983), which had pertinent proposals for the state. More than 40 percent of the fresh Plan was allotted to the agricultural sector and for rural development projects, reflecting an increase of over 100 percent allocation for the agricultural sector.

The relatively pertinent step was an attempt to relocate investment for the rural development projects by means of enhancing major and medium range irrigation schemes, land reforms, help to rural landless poor, block level planning and so on.

In the election manifesto of the Party, it was found that in both the years i.e. 1977 and 1980, the Party announced that it abides by the Gandhian path of development by giving priority to agricultural growth and development as opposed to the Nehruvian path of development initiated by the Congress party, which promoted heavy, capital-intensive industrialization.

By analyzing in political terms, such policy measures were designed to forward the interests of the 'small farmers' and very specifically, that of the small cultivators in the rural areas. The primary factors responsible for the collapse of the Janata Party in U.P. to carry out its agricultural programmes/planning and also to emerge as a strong party with a rural ideological base, remains in the fact that the different elements of the party had conflicting class bases resulting into different economic interests which were bound to be in conflict.

Bahujan Samaj Party (BSP): During the 1980s, BSP was formed which changed the political scenario of Uttar Pradesh. It was formed by Kanshi Ram, a scheduled caste from Ropar district of Punjab. He mobilized people and formed the backward and minority community employees' federation, comprising largely of government employees in 1978.

The ideology on which the party evolved is resting on the thinking of Kanshi Ram. From the late years of 1970s Kanshi Ram attempted to convey his ideas that, although there is democracy in India based upon adult franchise, yet in practicality, the country has been dominated by the Brahmin castes, who are only about 10-15 percent of the total population.

About the Congress party organization, Kanshi Ram believed that it is the Congress that has been the 'main political instrument' of the upper castes; although rest of the national political parties are also considered to be as equally 'brahminical' in nature.

Communist Parties: The already existing two communist parties in India have never ever been able to play any significant role in the state of U.P. In name of electoral support base, these communist parties find only minimal representation in the eastern districts of the state of U.P. In the early years of 1950s, the communist parties started with a strategy that appeared different from that of the Congress party.

This different strategy is reflected in the document adopted by the party in 1951, which the party later converted into its first election manifesto. This manifesto described Indian society as a strongly feudal society in nature and the Indian state as very loyal in defending the interests of the big landlords.

After the split in the CPI organization, one section of the party stood strongly for the land reforms as a strategy towards 'curbing feudal land relations' and formation of capitalist relations within the socio-economic structure of agrarian society in parts of rural India. The CPI appeared to be less critical of the Congress party's agrarian policies programmes and in the 1970s, CPI got closer to the Congress organization. The CPI (Marxist group) in contrast demanded more radical strategies and blamed the Congress of 'allying with landlords defrauding the tiller of the right to land'.

The distinct paths followed by the CPI and CPI (M) became evident in the 1970s and the differences also reflected in their election manifestoes. In 1980s, both groups of the communist parties appeared to become blatantly critical of the failure of the government in improving conditions of the rural poor.

Economic Reforms and Agricultural Development since 1990s

Electoral mobilization in the backdrop of agrarian issues has been a pertinent feature in the politics of the state of Uttar Pradesh. During the early 1990s, constant economic slowdown and building up of economic crisis, both acting on each other, have been seen as a feature of the economy of Uttar Pradesh.

Agricultural farming sector interests saw natural evaporation from political manifestoes with identity-based issues making their way into the state politics during the 1990s. Following this, the agrarian sector remained in constant neglect and pushed to background in the state of Uttar Pradesh. [9]

The three important developments to be noted during the course of the study include: firstly, the state of Uttar Pradesh during the 1990s experienced the growth of primordial identities into the political ferry; secondly, their transformational effect on the electoral processes and thirdly, the historical processes leading to the political economy of economic liberalization. [10]

The state of Uttar Pradesh during the early 1990s witnessed a drastic fall in its growth rate and collapse of its fiscal health, leading to a critical situation of financial crisis. It presents a picture of a backward state among the Union of Indian states that has seen a poor performance since the initiation of economic reforms. Economic development, which gained its speed for the first time since Independence and was noticed during the years of 1980s, had fallen steeply since the early 1990s and has not yet managed to recover fairly.

The state of U.P. is placed among the BIMARU (characterized as backward and underdeveloped states, Bihar, Madhya Pradesh, Rajasthan and Uttar Pradesh) states. The state of U.P. also lags behind the states of Rajasthan and Madhya Pradesh, which have been performing considerable better over the last decade.

Various popular debates on the political economy of development in India have focused on the fact that is important for understanding among the interest-based and identity-based nature of politics on one hand and the political economy of development on the other hand. This also shows the capacity and power of the state to perform developmental actions along with effective governance. In the recent post-Independence era, intellectuals have addressed the capacity of the state to build a mixed economy that could enable the path of faster growth aligned with distributive justice.

Since the late 1980s, interest of the social scientists has moved to examination of the strength of the Indian State in implementation of the economic reforms. Few of the important debates are significant in order to understand the economic crisis in the state of Uttar Pradesh.

The emergence of distinct identities in the political sphere assisted with the rising demands on the state, on the one hand and the initiation of economic liberalization on the other hand together have taken toll at the same time, resulting in far reaching ramifications for the state autonomy and its strength. This has an important impact for the way in which the duty of the state and its association with various societal sections is understood and conceptualized.

It is essential to take a note, that, some eminent economists have argued that, the higher growth rates in the liberal market-based economy leading to an unregulated economy in a democratic polity requires important safety measures that would benefit the poorer sections—the economic reforms are not reflecting the interests of the poorer sections.

But, the hypothesis of this study is that economic reforms have brought significant benefits for the well-off sections. This has resulted in increased class inequalities and regional disparities along with being hurtful for the poorer sections of the society. This shows that economic liberalization has definitely increased regional disparities.

In view of the backdrop of the above debate, social scientists and economists have reflected on the autonomy of the Indian state in promoting economic reforms. Ashutosh Varshney, has argued that, economic reforms have been forced in those selective areas that caters to the interests of the dominant classes of the areas, while the provisions that may impact the mass political base and may have negative outcomes, have been avoided.

On the other hand, there are various social scientists that argue that the Indian state had the potential to carry out these free market-based liberal economic reforms. The Rajiv Gandhi government during the mid-1980s had promoted a new group of civil servants trained at international institutions like the World Bank and they were people who were the believers in the neo-liberal ideas and were not limited by the societal pressures, to induct significant changes like bringing in industries based on modern technologies and free market forces, thus making the path clear for the economic reforms in 1991 much smoother.

During the period of late 1990s, Pranab Bardhan, examined the important changes that took place over a period of time in the organizational structure of the state and social classes, along with the impact of such changes on liberal economic reforms.

With the growth of neo-liberal ideas and the promotion of economic reforms, new ways of conceptualization of state governance developed in debates on development during the 1990s in India.

However, along with the promotion of broad- based structures of governance, that could provide for bigger room for free market forces along with the civil society, the state institutions remained core to the processes of development. This is specifically true for states like Uttar Pradesh that has merely been touched by liberalized economic reforms. The Human Development Report of U.P. had listed such areas where the involvement of the state apparatus can be limited; this was done by curbing the fiscal deficit that would result in improved methods of governance (Human Development Report U.P., 2005).

However, besides these, other attempts to bring privatization and closing of the sick public sector enterprises along with the promotion of a new industrial policy measures to bring in the industrial capital during the late 1990s were not taken by the preceding governments (at most these were only best implemented partially).

Reforms in Agriculture

Economic reforms in India have been condemned for being completely concentrated on industrial development and globalization of commercial policies, thus eliminating agricultural progression and innovation, a segment that still offers employment to fifty five percent of the Indian populace. Dramatic reduction in the levels of agricultural production and its contribution to national income makes the critical arguments of social scientists quite apparent.

This weakening in agrarian performance is mainly due to a strident fall in the sums of public investments made in farming, such as irrigation, drainage, formal regulated market measures and institutions, rural infrastructure in terms of roads, electricity and so on.

As suggested by Gulati and Bhalla (2001), "this decline began much before the reforms and was actually sharper in the 1980s than in the 1990s...they also point out that while public investment declined this was more than offset by a rise in private investment in agriculture which accelerated after the reforms".

Though, there is no doubt about the significance of financing in farming sector, but given the socio-economic situation, this financing has to come from the state as the private investment is challenging to aid agriculture in its growth. Certainly, the privatization trend in farming could diminish its overall progress, where more than ninety percent of cultivators are poor and have livelihood earning complications.

The main reason why public financing for agrarian and rural sector failed is due to the bad financial balance sheet and monetary crisis of the state government. This directed to the normally accepted belief of progression of private investment in the industrial sector of the economy, which would ultimately escalate the production and income generation in the country.

And this means the apparent and forceful withdrawal of state subsidized support for agriculture. Another imperative repercussion of transformations within the agrarian sector is that it is the big and rich cultivators who would be benefitting from the scenario of liberalization, nevertheless, that may be for brief phase of time. Ultimately contract farming and privatization would substitute the survival cultivation, phasing out farmers and transforming them to wage labourers.

Liberalization has forced the state to withdraw itself from capitalizing into agriculture expansion, and encouraged private players to take the responsibility. In such a situation, small and marginal cultivators are the ones who are either trapped in huge debts or are forced to trade off their lands to capitalists in order to earn their living.

Rich cultivators are still accomplished of investing private money in farming and instead of trading their lands off; they are contracting it out to superior industrial capitalists. Though, there is a catch here, like capitalists continuously function on the norm of profit maximization, here too, the land will be used to farm those crops which will make enormous profits and will also get unprotected against substantial pesticides and fertilizers which will over the phase of time, harm its configuration and hence its productiveness.

Consequently, the agricultural sector requires a thorough strategy attention for its liberation from the capitalized market economy. International global market competition is constructed on certain set biases. Indian economic policy makers have botched to identify or have intentionally overlooked the fact that, in all advanced and capitalist states, farming is highly sheltered and is a profit-making employment/profession.

It is due to evident policy easing by their regimes, where not only in the domestic market but also in the international market agrarian crop from capitalist states is appropriately compensated. Thanks to the World Trade Organization (WTO) contracts, where the emerging states are obliged to remove subsiding their farming and capitalists states are greatly supporting their agriculture (this is very much evident by the Blue and Green Box subsidies of WTO).

This ultimately generates extremely imbalanced international market provisions, leading to cheap agrarian harvests from the developing nations. In India, now-a-days, the nature of competitive politics also makes it problematic to reorganize subsidies and generate state agrarian support.

In its place, the state has pressed in those policy measures, which takes the Indian farming to global bazaars without any shield. For example, the Bt cotton case, where farmers were made passionate about the cotton farming, which would obtain them enormous revenues and eradicate their poverty. In the entire exercise of cotton production, starting from the inputs used to post-production deeds, poor cultivator took hefty credits only to return into an enormous debt trap due to crash in worldwide global market prices.

The report of Task Force on Employment, which was lately shaped by the Government of India, made inclusive endorsements for evaluation of several other outmoded agricultural regulations (Planning Commission, 2001). For illustration, laws deliberated to protect land rentiers—this is a significant policy objective, which will discourage small cultivators from marketing or even leasing out their lands to larger agriculturalists in fear of being not adept to reclaim the land from the rentier.

Additional such policy measures like the introduction of Agricultural Produce Marketing Acts in many states, will direct buyers to buy any farming harvest in a controlled market. The aim is to forbid the commercial dealers from amassing the farming harvest or to make any contractual association with the cultivators. Though, such measures have demonstrated to be of petite help as they are deficient in infrastructure and implementing organizations.

Agrarian Crisis and Rural Distress

The Bundelkhand area in Uttar Pradesh has observed industrial backwardness for a very long period of time. The province is dominantly reliant upon its agricultural economy. Though lately, an epidemic of farmers' suicides in the province has raised significant questions. It is perceived that farming in the Bundelkhand area has been abandoned by both the State as well as the Central government by ignoring essential issues such as farm dilapidation, transformation of farming and rural indebtedness.

Bundelkhand is a province with rich environmental reserves and fossils, yet the area is in suffering and inching towards a catastrophe. The economic backwardness of the province remains unexplored. A field study done in the Bundelkahnd area of Uttar Pradesh reveals that suffering in the area could not be elucidated by the abnormality of rainy season and other environmental factors.

There lies hidden policy related structural problems; along with traditionally/historically determined/constructed social associations of production, and multifaceted connections between caste and land ownership in the province. Now-a-days, along with the existence of above mentioned factors, the most imperative is the "implications" brought in via economic reforms and liberal free market philosophy upon farming in India.

The movement of Indian economy from socialist welfare to free market capitalist economy after 1991 has been demonstrated to carry in stark results for the agricultural sector. The field study in Bundelkhand province throws some stimulating insights on how cultivators are under enormous debts.

Prior to economic liberalization, farm economy was receiving a lot of state provided inducements in terms of agricultural subsidies and other such measures. The new economic policy espoused by the Indian State headed to the removal of agricultural subsidies and other such measures to a huge degree. This made the Indian cultivators vulnerable in the free market sphere. The field study describes their story in Bundelkhand region as to how agriculture has become a grief for them.

To comprehend the nature of stark influence of the economic reforms upon cultivation in rural Bundelkahnd province, it is significant to know the variations in the fundamental agricultural structure.

The landowning agrarian populace of Bundelkhand province can be distributed into five clusters, i.e., big landholders; rich farmers; mid level peasants; small farmers and marginal cultivators (these classifications are both empirical, i.e., based on size dissemination of operating holdings and use of workforce, as well as non-quantified agricultural features). Big proprietors possess more than ten hectares of land.

They use rented labour rather than family workforce and frequently rent out land. Big proprietors extract excess in the form of rental charge of their land. While in certain areas, big proprietors have in current years accepted the new technology, nevertheless, yet most of them still use pre-capitalist techniques of extricating excess like renting out their land for a secure sum of payment.

The other class of rich farmers own generally around four to ten hectares of land. They are self-cultivating agrarians who frequently rent in land to raise their holdings. They use domestic as well as hired workforce specifically throughout peak agrarian months of the year. The chief features of this class are the acceptance and implementation of new farm technology i.e., high yielding varieties of seeds, tractors, burrowing of tube-wells etc.

Middle farmers are those who possess two to four hectares of land. They are often part possessors and part renters, that is, they tend to use fewer rented and more of their private family workforce and not have been capable to implement the new technology.

Small and marginal cultivators are those who work on one to two hectares of land and also occasionally below one hectare correspondingly.

All of them are renters and cannot have enough money for any outside workforce. The majority of them comprise the class of farming labourers. They are carrying on existence farming and constitute the poorest segment of the agricultural class pyramid. It is essential to note that numerically they comprise of the biggest group.

What is significant to note here is that, however the separations of agricultural classes are quite well defined, it is also replicating a specific kind of political economy of the province? It is observed that none of the classes amid agricultural sector remains unaltered by the pro neo-liberal economic reforms.

The big proprietors and rich agriculturalists belong to this class and have been least disturbed due to commencement of economic reforms as they do not cultivate their private land and give it on lease to landless workers.

It is the small and landless workers that have come to tolerate the brunt of the market forces in its wickedest form (to the extent that suicides have become a common feature of this class in recent times).

In theory, the liberal policies introduced by the Indian state entails rolling back most of the significant input grants delivered to the farming sector. The field study in the Bundelkahnd section has covered four districts viz., Mahoba, Banda, Hamirpur and Jhansi and recounts the first hand account of how small and marginal cultivators have been trapped into the vicious circle of free market forces.

The slowdown in farming and weakness of the rural sector came obvious from the examination of disaster of livelihoods and lives for the cultivators in the region. In informal interviews conducted with several cultivators of four different districts, the following principal aspects of the catastrophe distressing scenario for farmers are discussed.

With the opening up of the economy to the international markets, opportunities of export openings and higher world prices for farming commodities led many cultivators to move into cash crops (that is a shift towards commercial agriculture) in the Bundelkahnd province (away from the traditional subsistence crops).

This change has been a costly business for all the cultivators and predominantly small and marginal cultivators. In hope of reaping good profits through profitable commercial farming, cultivators were encouraged by several government policies and agendas to undertake the risk.

In a conversation with a group of cultivators in Mahoba district, it was observed that in order to encourage cash crops, large number of cultivators undertook hefty credits to meet their input expenses.

For an illustration, as they recalled, "the Mayawati Government in Uttar Pradesh in 2008, encouraged the cultivators to grow cash crops by providing agrarian credit to poor farmers". The deflation of Rupee made Indian exports inexpensive and hence appealing to the world market.

The Uttar Pradesh state government during the decade of 2000 encouraged the cultivators in Bundelkhand province to grow cash crops by offering enticements/incentives in the form of rebates on HYV seeds and pesticides.

Even in parched areas that were inappropriate for cash crops like oilseeds and cotton cultivation, the cultivators were asked for this shift. The poor cultivators of Bundelkhand area got attracted to large profits from HYV seeds and export openings. This resulted in several cultivators giving up their conventional survival farming in favour of cash crops.

Cash crops, mainly the HYVs are reliant on heavy inputs, as they need larger amount of water, fertilizers and pesticides to cultivate and to harvest the predictable productivity.

With the start of economic reforms that was trailed by market economy, the state grants on these inputs had previously weakened. The market prices of these inputs had shot up resulting in severe rise in the overall cost of production.

Paradoxically, following the change from existence farming to water intensive cash crops, the state governments totally abandoned the financing of surface irrigation infrastructure (the U.P. State Planning and Statistical Department shows no investment during the period 1997-2010 in irrigation sector of Bundelkhand province).

As a consequence, the big proprietors were required to make private financing in generating their private wells and fixing of electric motors. This also resulted in manipulation and misappropriation of the ground water.

The cost of fitting and upkeep of electric motors and politics of water delivery were forced on poor renters in the form of extraction of maximum sum of charge, leading to greater cost of cultivation. Thirdly, the steady elusion of state sustenance also meant that numerous state run corporations that had provided support to the poor cultivators and renters became non-existent.

In the state, the U.P. State Agro Development Corporation, which was helping in manufacturing and dissemination of farming machinery, implements and other inputs at minutest rates, got vanished. With the vanishing of such institutes, the private players in the province appeared and took up their roles.

Marginal, small and poor cultivators opined that nearly 99 percent of small and landless cultivators are under debt. This displays that a definite kind to capitalist class have appeared, who did not have any prime interests of the cultivators at the centre of their business accomplishments.

The abandonment of the state sustenance was most intensely felt by the cultivators due to the failure of the organized credit provision in the area. Consequently, it can be said that, this has caused enormous rural indebtedness for the Bundelkhand agrarians and is one of the principal causes of suffering and underdevelopment of farming in the region.

From the inputs costs side, it is consequently unearthed that economic reforms programme resulted in an extraordinary increase in input farm costs.

In Bundelkhand area, fertilizers subsidies have been removed. The supply of fertilizers has been passed on to the private sector mediators. Additional observation is that, the price of agricultural credit has also augmented substantially.

The treatment of farming as an important sector for offering loans at low interest rates from the banking system has vanished.

Cultivators belonging to marginal and small agricultural classes in Banda district of Bundelkhand region of U.P. opined that, "all of them took credits and the sum of loans they took to produce cash crops was much higher than they had taken in the past".

Consequently, the switch to an exportable profitable commercial crops steered to a scenario of increasing indebtedness amongst the Bundelkhand agrarians.

Uttar Pradesh government in 2000s did not interfere with any valorization plans like procurement of unsold cash crops at a fair price from the cultivators. The state government could have done so, but it was functioning with the norm of parting everything to the free market.

The change in the cropping pattern with the institution of capitalist free market practices in cultivation has no hesitation in bringing chaos among the cultivators in the Bundelkhand region. Commercial farming of water intensive crops like cotton and wheat means rising demands for scarce water resources.

Where an area is identified for its lack of water resources and has often observed drought, the area is not good for commercial crops. Now-a-days, the cultivators have intentionally shifted towards commercial cropping.

This has resulted in abolition of existence agriculture and shortage of necessities for a majority of the populace, especially lower castes, landless and the poor. People in diverse villages have been left to fend for themselves for essential necessities of life viz., nutrition, drinking water, health, education and social security.

The concluding comments about the grief and distress in the rural Bundelkhand region can be recapitulated in following points.

Firstly, the field study to Bundelkhand has conveyed one certain remark, i.e., the level of underdevelopment and agricultural catastrophe cannot be just elucidated by meek absenteeism of monsoon rains as has been observed by the state and the Central government. Secondly, there are long-term structural problems connected to government policies and programmes.

Along with this, social association of production in the area too are accountable for the underdevelopment of farming—the presence of highly unsatisfactory distribution of land amongst agricultural classes, the close association of caste and land possession, as well as abandonment of agricultural renovation in the area during the Green Revolution period.

Lastly, with the commencement of economic reforms, the state support for the farming sector was withdrawn and the resultant exposure of farm sector to open market functions. Thirdly, the poor and landless got stuck in an excruciating vicious debt cycle forcing many of them to migrate to cities to earn livelihood, where they are exposed to additional weak conditions of poor life.

Hence, the nature of disaster in Bundelkhand is illustrative of a picture of abandonment and discrimination by the state. In the end it can be said that, there are certain ambiguities connected with liberal market economy concerning agriculture in India, which greets commercial farming and abandonment of state support.

A government that concerns just about the growth rates of the economy cannot and will not appear to glare into explanations/causes for the catastrophe in agriculture.

Conclusion

The state of Uttar Pradesh has experienced significant changes in the agrarian society and that has its roots in the history of development trajectory. The state of Uttar Pradesh marked with regional disparities in its climate and the condition of the soil composition, in particular between Gangetic plains and Bundelkhand, Oudh and the eastern north-west provinces, are characterized by these environmental conditions.

The influence of monsoon over the life and death of the land cultivators has stood very apparent. The modern Indian history has provided enough evidence of making the region, specific with disparities in agricultural conditions.

Evidently, the British government implied that considerable backing (aid) was a prerequisite to the solution. However, the present problems of agriculture find its roots in the history of development and assistance.

By the means of the use of the then modern doctrines of the British engineering to utilize the ignored reserves of the Ganges and the Yamuna for a massive system of waterways to irrigate the desiring soils of the conventionally and inherently very prolific Doab, navigation canals for the swifter supply of its impressively augmented harvest were offered.

In an era of around twenty five years from the beginning of the pronounced Ganga canal in 1854, the second and biggest canal structure in India and of the planet before, some 5,601 miles of core water rows and distributaries had been built, covering an anticipated watered area in 1887-88 of approximately 1,500,000 acres in the western districts of the state of Uttar Pradesh. The ingenuous aim of the building of the waterways was to obtain greatest income from conventionally beneficial areas of farming in the state.

In addition to the demanding agrarian production matters, there also existed the concern of income generation in the state. Initiated by the British government, the revenue paying costs from the cultivators was that of the concern for credit, rent and debt and has remained ever since that time.

Agriculture even in the current liberal economy continues to be the strength of the Indian economy and sadly at present is at its weakest form. The current study conveys out a picture portraying deprived scenario in the field of agriculture via its reduced contribution to the Indian GDP, which at one point of time was the chief contributor.

The study discovered numerous concerns like low accessibility of technical assistance for the cultivators; low yield-producing seeds, scarcity of storage amenities, minimum support prices, insignificant irrigation system, non-existence of proper credit delivery channels and insufficient protective cover that shields agriculture from overall consequence of liberalization.

Small and marginal cultivators have been the poorest sufferers due to the dynamics of free market liberal economic policies.

Nevertheless, the appropriate question is whether Indian agriculture has been able to profit from the structural modification or it is confronting any suffering under demands placed upon it by liberalization, privatization and new economic policies.

Endnotes

1. Baljit Singh and Mishra (1190), "A Study of Land Reforms in U.P.", Oxford Book Co.

2. A recent study found that 70 percent of U.P. is cultivated by farmers owing less than 4 hectare of land and 6 percent by those with more than 10 hectares. "The Economy of U.P.", in 'The Economies of the Indian Union' (ed.) (2008), M.S. Adiseshiah, Lancer International, New Delhi.
3. Sheila Bhalla (1998), "New Relations of Production in Northern Indian Agriculture", *Economic and Political Weekly*, March.
4. T.J. Byres (1981), "The New Technology, Class Formation and Class Action in the Countryside", *Journal of Peasant Studies*, Volume 8, No. 4, July.
5. L.I. Rudolph and S.H. Rudolph (1986), "Determinants and Varieties of Agrarian Mobilization", in Meghnad Desai (ed.), 'Agrarian Power and Agricultural Productivity in South Asia', Oxford University Press, New Delhi.
6. Terry J. Byres (1972), "The Dialectic of India's Green Revolution", *South Asia Review*, January.
7. Government of India (1988), Ministry of Home Affairs, Research and Policy Division, "Causes and Nature of Agrarian Tensions", Report.
8. Paul Brass (1968), "Uttar Pradesh in State Politics in India", (ed.), Myron Weiner, Princeton University.
9. Francine, Francine R. (eds.), (2000), "Transforming India: Social and Political Dynamics of Democracy", New Delhi, Oxford University Press.
10. Corbridge, Stuart and John Harriss (2000), "Reinventing India: Liberalization, Hindu Nationalism, and Popular Democracy", Cambridge UK: Polity Press.

Bibliography

Bibliography

Acharya, S.S. and Papanek, G.F. (1995), "Explaining Agricultural Wage Trends in India", *Development Policy Review*, Vol. 13, No. 1, March.

Ahluwalia, M.S. (1978), "Rural Poverty and Agricultural Performance in India", *Journal of Development Studies*, Vol. 14(3), April.

Ahluwalia, M.S. (1986), "Rural Poverty, Agricultural Production and Prices", in J.W. Mellor and G.M Desai (eds.), 'Agricultural Change and Rural Poverty', Oxford University Press: New Delhi.

Ahluwalia, Montek Singh, "New Economic Policy and Agriculture: Some Reflection", *Indian Journal of Agricultural Economics*, 51(3) July-September 1996.

Alagh, K.Y. (1998-99), "Agricultural Trade and Policies", *Indian Economic Journal*, January-March, Vol. 46, No. 3, p. 56.

Baden Powell, B.H. (1971), "The Indian Village Community", Delhi: Cosmo Publications.

Badge, R.K. and Kalava, A. (1998), "Agriculture: Changing Trends in IT", XII National Conference of Agriculture Research Statisticians, proceedings, pp. 171-175.

Bahaduri, Amit (1973), "A Study in Agricultural Backwardness under Semi-Feudalism", *Economic Journal*, March, LXXXIIT: pp. 120-137.

Balakrishnan (2000), "Agriculture and Economic Reforms, Growth and Welfare", *Economic and Political Weekly*, Vol. 35, No. 12.

Batia, M.S. (1999), "Rural Infrastructure and Growth in Agriculture", *Economic and Political Weekly,* Vol. 34, March 27.

Betaille, Andre (1977), "Studies in Agrarian Social Structure", Delhi: Oxford University Press.

Bhalla, G.S. and Gurmit Singh (1997), "Recent Developments in Indian Agriculture: A State Level Analysis", *Economic and Political Weekly*, March 29-April 4.

Bhalla G.S. and Tyagi G.S. (1989), "Patterns in Indian Agricultural Development: A District Level Study", New Delhi: Institute for Studies in Industrial Development.

Bhalla G.S. (2000), "Emerging Crisis in Indian Agriculture: Causes and Suggested Remedies", *Mainstream*, Annual, December 23.

Bharadwaj, K. (1974), "Production Conditions in Indian

Agriculture", London: Cambridge University Press.

Brown, D.D. (1971), "Agricultural Development in India's Districts", Cambridge: Harvard.

Chadha, G.K. (2003), "Indian Agriculture in the New Millennium: Human Response to Technology Challenges", *Indian Journal of Agricultural Economics,* January-March.

Chaudhri D.P. (1998), "Agrarian Reform and Agrarian Reformation", New Delhi, Sage Publications.

Dattatreyulu (1988), "India's Agricultural Exports", *Foreign Trade Review,* Vol. 23.

Desai, A.R. (ed.) (1979), "Peasant Struggles in India", Bombay: Oxford University Press.

Dorner, Peter (1972), "Land Reform and Economic Development", England: Modern Penguin.

Dreze, Jean and Amartya Sen (1995), "Indian Economic Development and Social Opportunity", Oxford University Press, New Delhi.

Etienne, G. (1968), "Studies in Indian Agriculture: The Art of the Possible", Berkeley: University Press.

Fry Kenberg, R.C. (ed.) (1961), "Land Control and Social Structure in Indian History", Madison: Madison University Press.

Ghose, K.K. (1969), "Agricultural Labourers in India", Calcutta: Indian Publications.

Ghosh, M. (1996), "Agricultural Development and Rural Poverty in India", *Indian Journal of Agricultural Economics,* Vol. 51.

Government of India, Ministry of Agriculture and Farmers Welfare, *Annual Report* (various years).

Gulati, Ashok (1998), "Indian Agriculture in an Open Economy: Will it Prosper?", in Isher Judge Ahluwalia and I.M.D. Little (eds.), 'India's Economic Reforms and Development: Essays for Manmohan Singh', Oxford University Press, New Delhi.

Gulati, Ashok (1996), "Reforms and Policies for Agriculture", in Vijay L. Kelkar and V.V. Bhanoji Rao (eds.), 'Development Policy Imperatives', Tata McGraw-Hill, New Delhi.

Gulati, Ashok and Anil Sharma (1995), "Subsidy Syndrome in Indian Agriculture", *Economic and Political Weekly*, Review of Agriculture, XXX (39), September 30.

Gulati, Ashok and Kelly, Tim (1999), "Trade Liberalization and Indian Agriculture", Oxford University Press, New Delhi.

Gulati, Ashok (1996), "New Economic Policy and Indian Agriculture", *Indian Journal of Agricultural Economics,*

January-June.

Gupta, S.C. (1963), "Agrarian Relations and Early British Rule in India Ceded and Conquered Areas", New Delhi: Asia Publishing House.

Himanshu, B. and A. Sen (2011), "Why Not a Unified Food Security Legislation?", *Economic and Political Weekly,* Vol. 46, April.

Jetley, Surinder (1977), "Modernising Indian Peasants", India: Asian Educational Services.

Jha, D. (2001), "Agriculture Research and Small Farmers", Presidential Address, 60th Annual Conference of Indian Society of Agricultural Economics, Institute for Studies in Population, Agricultural and Rural Change, University of Kalyani, Kalyani.

Joshi, P.C. (1976), "Land Reforms in India", Delhi: Allied Publishers.

Kalra, O.P. and C.S. Jain (1994), "Agricultural Policy in India", *Journal of Agricultural Economics*, August.

Konar, D.N. (1997), "Trend of Indian Agriculture in the Post-Independence Period', *Artha Beekha*, Vol. 6, No. 2, December.

Krishnaiah, M. (1995), "Labour Institutions in Backward Agriculture", in R. Radhakrishna and Alakh N. Sharma (eds.), 'Empowering Rural Labour in India', New Delhi, Institute for Human Development.

Kumar, P. (2001), "Agricultural Performance and Productivity", in S.S. Acharya and P. Chaudhari (eds.), 'Indian Agricultural Policy', New Delhi: Rawat Publications.

Mahendradev, S. (1996), "Medium and Long-term Implications for Indian Agriculture and Linkages to OECD Countries", Paper Written for OECD, Paris.

Millikan and Hapgood (eds.) (1967), "No Easy Harvest: The Dilemma of Agriculture in Underdeveloped Countries", Boston Little Brown.

Misra, S. (ed.) (1965), "Major Sources of Irrigation in U.P.", Delhi: Oxford and IBH.

National Bank for Agriculture and Rural Development (NABARD), *Annual Report* (various years).

Nayyar, Deepak and Sen, Abhijit (1994), "International Trade and the Agricultural Sector in India", *Economic and Political Weekly*, May 14.

Niti Aayog (2015), "Raising Agricultural Productivity and Making Farming Remunerative for Farmers".

Pawan Kumar (2006), "Rural Infrastructure: Thrust Area in Rural Development", *Kurukshetra,* Vo. 54, No. 9.

Radhakrishna, R. (2002), "Food and Nutrition Security" in Kirit S. Parikh and R. Radhakrishna (eds.), 'India Development Report, 2002', Oxford University Press.

Rao, Hanumantha C.H. (1995), "Liberalization of Agriculture in India: Some Major Issues", *Indian Journal of Agricultural Economics*, Vol. 3.

Rao, Hanumantha C.H. (1999), "Changing Economic Structure of the Rural Economy in Asia and the Pacific", paper presented at the study meeting on Rural Transformation, held at Yogakarta, Indonesia, November 29 to December 3.

Rao, Hanumantha C.H. (2001), "WTO and Viability of Indian Agriculture", *Economic and Political Weekly*, September 8.

Rao, Hanumantha C.H. (2003), "Reform Agenda for Agriculture", *Economic and Political Weekly*, Vol. 8, No. 7.

Reserve Bank of India, *Bulletin* (various issues).

Sharma, Pardeep and Gulati, Ashok (1995), "WTO and Indian Agriculture", *Economic and Political Weekly*, March 10.

Subramanian, Shankar (1993), "Agricultural Trade Liberalisation and India", Paris: Development Centre Studies, OECD.

Thamarajakshi, R. (1999), "Agriculture and Economic Reforms", *Economic and Political Weekly*, Vol. 34, No. 33.

Thorner, Daniel (1956), "The Agrarian Prospect in India", Delhi: Delhi University Press.

Timothy, Josling (1998), "Agricultural Trade Policy: Completing the Reform", Institute for International Economics.

United Nations (1951), "Land Reforms: Defects in Agrarian Structure as Obstacles to Economic Development", New York.

Vaidyananthan, A. (2000), "Indian Agriculture Policy", *Economic and Political Weekly*, Vol. 35 No. 10.

Vyas, V.S. (2001), "Agriculture: Second Round of Economic Reforms", *Economic and Political Weekly*, Vol. 36, No. 10.

Vyas, V.S., "WTO and Indian Agriculture", Agricultural Science Section, at the 88th Session of the Indian Science Congress, Indian Agricultural Research Institute, New Delhi.

Websites

Ministry of Agriculture and Farmers Welfare

Ministry of Rural Development

Ministry of Panchayati Raj
Ministry of Water Resources, River Development and Ganga Rejuvenation
Ministry of Chemicals and Fertilizers
Ministry of Food Processing Industries
Ministry of Finance
Ministry of Environment, Forest and Climate Change
Reserve Bank of India
National Bank for Agriculture and Rural Development (NABARD)
Niti Aayog

Index

Index